A Small Town in Texas

Texas Heritage Series
Number Four

Also in this series:

Christmas at the Ranch by Elmer Kelton
What I Learned on the Ranch by James Bruce Frazier
The Parramore Sketches by Dock Dilworth Parramore

This book is dedicated to my brother, Charlie,
and to the memory of our parents,
Glenn A. and Minnie Lee Dromgoole

A Small Town in Texas

Reflections on growing up in the '50s and '60s

Glenn Dromgoole

Cover painting by Charlie Hukill

State House Press
McMurry University
Abilene, Texas

Library of Congress Cataloging-in-Publication Data

Dromgoole, Glenn.
    A small town in Texas : reflections on growing up in
    the '50s and '60s / Glenn Dromgoole.
    p. cm. -- (Texas heritage series ; no. 4)
    ISBN 1-880510-86-3 (alk. paper)
    1. Sour Lake (Tex.)--Social life and customs--20th centu-
ry. 2. Dromgoole, Glenn--Childhood and youth. 3. Sour Lake
(Tex.)--Biography. 4. Nineteen fifties. 5. Nineteen sixties.
I. Title. II. Series.
    F394.S696D76 2004
    976.4'157--dc22

                                        2004011815

State House Press
McMurry Station, Box 637
Abilene, TX 79697-0637
(325) 793-4682
www.mcwhiney.org

Printed in the United States of America

1-880510-86-3
10 9 8 7 6 5 4 3 2 1

Book Designed by Rosenbohm Graphic Design

Contents

All photographs are from the author's personal collection.

Introduction

The past lives in us, not we in the past. –David Ben-Gurion

This is a book about the past, but also about the present. It is about growing up in the '50s and '60s in a small town in Texas. That's the setting, the background for the stories and essays collected here.

But it is not a memoir as such, for the important thing here is not so much one person's experiences—mine —but how society has changed in the past half century and how perhaps in other ways it hasn't.

When I write about growing up in a segregated society, that is a commentary on the past but also a prologue to the present. A personal essay on my grandparents is, on a larger scale, a connection to values that grandparents still try to communicate today. A piece about my favorite toy lies in con-trast to the expensive gizmos we lavish on our children today.

The stories in this book are autobiographical, in that they draw on my own journey, but they do not constitute an autobiography. Rather, they are one man's commentary intersecting the past with the present and exploring what may be of lasting value.

The setting for most of these stories is a little town in Texas by the odd name of Sour Lake, population sixteen hundred or so in the '50s, in the '60s, in the '70s, and even today. The town, about fifteen miles west of Beaumont and seventy miles east of Houston, has neither withered up like many small towns nor experienced the uncontrolled growth of other towns, especially those close to metropolitan areas.

But that is not to say that it has remained the same. Although its population hasn't changed much, Sour Lake has experienced the sociological tremors felt by the rest of the world. It has been forever affected and altered by television, urban migration, increased opportunities for women and minorities, changing family lifestyles, the computer age. The Sour Lake I grew up in is no more the Sour Lake of today than the America of the '50s is the America of today.

This is a different world, and in many ways a much better one. I am not one who worships nostalgia. If I grew up in an age of innocence, it was certainly not an age of purity. We had simply not yet begun—or were just beginning—to confront the issues and problems that lay beneath the seemingly placid surface of everyday life.

Looking back on it, I remember life as being good, for the most part. But it wasn't so good for everyone. The slice of American pie that I found so sweet would leave a bitter taste in the mouths of many Americans.

Still, there are certain values that remain true today, values that have shaped my life and continue to shape people's lives in the twenty-first century, whether they come from Sour Lake, Texas, or New York City. Values like friendship, love, encouragement, kindness, courtesy, civility, honesty, humor, faith, responsibility, courage, community, family. Values we have benefited from. Values we can cherish. Values we can pass along.

I invite you to join me in reliving these simpler times and exploring these enduring values.

Perhaps these reflections will engage your own memories and encourage you to share your stories and insights about what you have learned from your pilgrimage. That would, indeed, be the highest compliment.

Up from the Fifties

I wasn't a baby boomer myself. I was born in 1944, and the baby boom didn't officially begin until 1946. When we graduated from high school in our small Texas town, our class had fifty-two students. The class two years later, the first of the baby boomers, had more than a hundred.

Still, we were on the fringes of the post-war generation that grew up in the '50s. And while the '50s were simpler times, they were also changing times. The changes didn't hit full force until the '60s, but they were starting to ferment in the '50s.

• Television had become part of our lives, opening up all kinds of possibilities and experiences—some good, some bad.

• Music was erupting with not only a new beat aimed at younger people, those newly termed "teen-agers," but a new language and a new culture as well.

• Blacks and Hispanics had fought in the War, and they were no longer willing to settle for second-class citizenship in the country for which they had put their lives on the line.

• Colleges were about to burst at the seams because of the sheer numbers of students in the post-war boom years.

• Churches had enjoyed a big revival in the early '50s, but by the late '50s people had begun to find other diversions.

• The migrations to the cities and suburbs had begun, as jobs shifted from rural to urban areas.

• Extended families were breaking up as people moved away from their roots to take better-paying jobs.

• Neighborhoods changed as housing was built farther and farther from downtown centers.

• On a scale never before realized, young people took to the streets in their cars. No other generation of adults had been affluent enough to afford cars for their children.

So what seemed like a peaceful and serene time, the decade of the '50s was in fact the calm before the storm. The storm broke loose in the '60s, and not just because of Vietnam. In fact, Vietnam was more of an effect of the '60s revolt than a cause of it.

We grew up with more freedom than any previous generation of young people had enjoyed. Some would say we were "spoiled," and perhaps they were right. We would question authority with a vengeance in the decades that were to come.

It's always fun to look back on one's growing-up years and romanticize about the "good old days." Certainly there were many, many wonderful things about the '50s. It was, indeed, a good time to be young. We sort of had the best of both worlds—the last vestiges of a more stable, secure, protective society and the beginning of a new era of freedom and opportunity.

Reflecting from the vantage of nearly five decades of hindsight, the '50s do not appear to be so much the last era of stability as the cradle of a revolution which would change us—as individuals and as a nation—forever.

A Generation in Blue Jeans

My dad wore "trousers." He never looked comfortable in jeans. I cannot recall my mother, or hardly anyone else's mother, wearing jeans when I was growing up. Even today, my mother-in-law does not own a pair of pants, much less jeans.

As much as anything, blue jeans became an outward symbol of what would be known as the "generation gap." Jeans represented a major shift in how America dressed, a change that has continued to this day. It marked a new informality, not just in dress but as an approach to life.

My generation and the generations that followed us have less of a gap, it seems to me, in our outlook on life.

We grew up listening to rock music. So did they.

We grew up wearing jeans and tennis shoes. So did they.

We grew up with less reverence for institutions and authority. So did they.

*In the summer, boys wore jeans and went barefoot,
even to Vacation Bible School.*

We may remember life without TV, but we grew up watching TV most of our lives. So did they.

We drove cars from the time we were old enough to take driver's ed. So did they.

We are not shocked by the language in the movies or on the street. Neither are they.

These were changes which were dramatic, maybe even radical, for the pre-World War II generations—our elders. Our parents listened to a different type of music than we did. They wore different clothes. They lived through the Depression and rationing and fought the War and learned to sacrifice. They respected authority. They watched their language.

Thanks to them, we were the first generation of prosperity. We have had it pretty easy, comparatively, all our lives. We were the first generation, some would say, to be "spoiled." We have, in turn, lavished even more possessions on our children and grandchildren. They are even more "spoiled," more materialistic than we were. They have even less respect for authority. They are less likely to be courteous and considerate and generous.

Basically, we understand them, for they are more like us than we were like our parents or grandparents. Even in our fifties or sixties, we still think of ourselves as young.

We may find these days that we have more respect for our parents' values, more reverence for their traditions, and more regard for their contributions. But we still like a good rock song. We still appreciate a dirty joke. We still are spoiled.

And we still wear jeans.

Black and White Worlds

It seems incredible to me now, but I did not know a single black child when I was growing up.

Black children lived just a few blocks from where I lived. They walked by my house every day on their way to town. We may have occasionally acknowledged each other's existence in passing, but it was like we lived in two different worlds.

And, in fact, we did. I lived in the white world of decent schools, nice houses, green lawns, bright futures. They lived in the black world of inadequate schools, dilapidated houses, hand-me-down clothing, few opportunities.

Growing up, I didn't understand until I was older that there was anything wrong with that. I went to church every week, Sundays and Wednesdays, and I'm sure I heard my dad, a minister, preach about racial injustice, because I know he did. But it didn't register with me until, oh, probably after I went off to college, that justice was more than just being nice and respectful toward people of color.

Like a lot of white people, the only black person I knew well was our cleaning lady. She came twice a week, once to clean, once to iron. Her name was Hattie Fisher, and I always called her by her first name, Hattie. I wouldn't have thought of calling older white women by their first names—and my parents most certainly would have corrected me if I had. But Mrs. Fisher was always Hattie. Different worlds.

Hattie was a large woman who smelled of snuff and sweat. Her spirit was a curious mixture of melancholy and merriment, reflecting the very real daily struggles of her life and yet the hope and faith she carried in her heart. She moved slowly and with great effort, but usually had a song on her lips which she half-whistled, half-hummed.

I liked Hattie, and I probably was around her more than any other adult except my parents. But I can't say that I really knew her. I knew where she lived, in "colored town." I knew that she didn't have a car and she either walked or we drove her to the grocery store. I knew that she took good care of me, that I felt safe and protected when she was around. But I didn't know her family. I knew she had a mother, Marie, again just her first name. I never knew her children; they may have been grown by that time, but I never saw pictures of them or ever talked with her about them. I didn't know how old she was, though one time I asked.

She had broached the subject. "Glenn Allen," she asked, "how old are you now?" "Six," I replied, "how old are you." She laughed but politely let me know that it was not an appropriate question for a child to ask an adult.

In some ways, Hattie was like a part of our family, which I've heard other white people say about their cleaning ladies. At noon she would stop work and sit with my parents to watch "As the World Turns." She and my dad joked a lot with each other. Mother treated her fairly and courteously and would insist that she eat with us at the table. But, of course, she wasn't family. At night she went to her world and we stayed in ours.

I don't recall white people in our town being mean to black people, or "colored people" as we called them when we were being polite. The "n" word was commonly heard, but not around our house, although one time my dad slipped. He had been working outside and came in the house with sweat pouring from him and exclaimed, "I've been working like a nigger." He stopped, incredulous at what he had said, and apologized profusely to Hattie. "Mr. Dromgoole," Hattie responded, "you don't have to be black to be a nigger."

But the enforced segregation of the day—more than the racial epithets—was, in fact, the worst kind of meanness. It labeled black people as second-class human beings, kept them poor and subservient, shut them off from opportunity, and denied them even the right to have a say in the government that ruled their lives.

In truth, we had not come all that far from slavery in that part of the country. So-called "separate but equal" was quite separate but hardly equal. The Supreme Court issued its landmark ruling on school desegregation in 1954, yet for all intents and purposes the ruling was ignored or snubbed for more than a decade.

The world was changing, and eventually our little town and the rest of the South would change, too. Just one generation later, my daughters would be astonished to hear how people had been considered legally "unequal." And when I look back on it now, it seems incredible that I didn't see anything wrong with that. It seems incredible that I didn't know any black children, even though they walked right by my house every day on their way to town.

When Busing
Wasn't a Bad Word

When I was in elementary school, even in junior high, it was a thrill to get to go home after school with my friend Mike Fritsche. Mike lived out in the country, and we would get to pick wild dewberries and go out to the stock tank and maybe ride horses or a tractor.

Mike only lived a couple of miles out of town, but back then it seemed a lot farther. Maybe it seemed farther because Mike rode the bus to school. So when I would go home with him after school, I would ride the bus with him.

I thought it was fun to ride the bus. Mike didn't particularly see the thrill in it because he had to ride it every day, twice a day. But to a boy who lived in town, riding the bus home was fun.

Back then no one thought of a school bus as controversial or symbolic. The bus simply brought the country kids to school. The bus was the way they could get an education. I don't remember anyone blaming the buses, much less cursing them, for bringing the country kids to our school.

A few years later, however, the yellow school bus came to have a different connotation. When the bus started bringing black kids to school, instead of country kids, all of a sudden "busing" became a bad word. At first, it was pretty simple racism: If you were opposed to busing, you pretty much had to be a racist because the only kids being bused were black.

But then it got more complicated. White kids got bused to what had been all-black schools, and black kids were bused to what had been all-white schools. Now even some "good" white folks, who would never utter the word "nigger" or admit they were prejudiced, were circulating petitions opposing busing.

In Fort Worth, where I was living in the late '60s, the school superintendent and school board, under court order, worked out a plan for fully integrating the elementary schools that seemed fair. It involved clustering three formerly white schools with one formerly black school. These clusters were set up all over town.

All children would attend their neighborhood schools in the first grade. The white kids would be bused to the black neighborhoods in the second grade, where all second graders would attend the formerly all-black schools. The black kids would be bused to the white neighborhoods in third, fourth and fifth grades. That would give all schools a roughly 75-25 mix of whites and minorities.

The situation could have been explosive, as it had been in other cities. But the school superintendent went all over the city promoting the plan. He talked to parents. He spoke to civic groups. He went on TV and explained how the plan would work. He met with the newspaper editorial board and wrote guest columns. He set up tours so parents could visit the schools their children would be attending. He promised the city that not only would this plan achieve full integration and satisfy the court order, it would result in a better educational program for all children. The newspaper and TV stations did a good job, also, of keeping people informed and urging reason and restraint.

Some parents circulated petitions opposing busing. A few threats were made. But on the first day of school, the buses rolled from black neighborhoods into white ones, and from white neighborhoods into black ones, and the kids went to school and there were few protests and no violence. Some parents held their children out of school for a few days, but soon enrollment was back to normal. White parents flocked to school receptions in neighborhoods they had previously gone out of their way to avoid. Black parents were welcomed to school receptions in neighborhoods where few black faces, other than household help, were commonly seen.

Busing worked then the way it had worked when Mike Fritsche rode the bus. It provided a safe, reliable, efficient way to get kids to school. How else could they get there?

The problem some folks had with busing never really had anything to do with school buses anyway. The problem wasn't the bus; it was fear of the unknown, fear that breeds prejudice and hate and violence.

A Man of Faith,
A Man of Courage

I have never considered myself a "born-again" Christian. I was born that way in the first place. Daddy was a Baptist minister, and our home revolved around the church.

But one religious experience always will stand out in my mind above all the rest. It made me know that religion was for real, that it mattered, that it truly could make a difference in people's lives. If I was "born again," it was then.

I was in college at the time. It was the summer between my junior and senior year, 1965, and I was working for a newspaper as a reporter intern and living at home. Little did I expect what was to take place that long, hot summer.

My three years away from home had taken me away from the church. After living with it every day for eighteen years, I had put it on the back burner in my life. But that summer something happened that would shape the life of the little town where I lived and would have a lasting impact on me.

Every summer, the first week of June, the church held its Vacation Bible School. We always had it the first week of June because, quite frankly, my father wanted to get it over with. Vacation Bible School was fun for the kids, but it was a headache for him.

That summer was different. Oh, Vacation Bible School was scheduled early in June as usual. But I have to back up a bit.

The decade of the '60s was when we finally came to grips with the fact that not all Americans were considered equal. I grew up with separate but equal, which was separate but hardly equal. People with dark skin went to inferior schools, worked at inferior jobs and lived in inferior homes. Equal rights were a farce, much less equal opportunity.

By the late '50s and early '60s that had begun to affect the conscience of the nation, even in the small towns of Texas. For several years before that summer—at least as early as 1954—Daddy had been preaching about the worth and dignity of the individual, regardless of race.

His sermons had begun to have some impact, and one Wednesday night the church leaders decided that the

Vacation Bible School that summer should be open to all children of the community. *All children*. The public schools would not be integrated until that fall, but Vacation Bible School would be integrated that summer.

So on the first day, several black children showed up. And several white church members, good Christian ladies, walked out. Before the day was over, their husbands were in my dad's office demanding his resignation. When he refused, they demanded a vote of the church.

He rose to his feet. "Gentlemen," he said, "I would welcome that!"

That was in June. The vote would not come until August. All summer the campaign went on, a campaign of anonymous letters, whispers, rumors, carefully-orchestrated hate.

Prejudice runs deep. My mother's best friend refused to have anything to do with her. My brother was playing Pony League baseball, and his coach was one of the most outspoken opponents of my dad. People who had been baptized by my dad, whose parents' funerals Daddy had preached, whose children he had married, turned on him.

He wrote a letter to one of the men in the church whom he had considered a "strong friend and supporter." The man had circulated a petition opposing him.

"I remember when you told me some years ago that when everybody else was against me, you would still be for me," he wrote the man.

"I am deeply hurt by your attitude," he continued, "and do not think I will recover from it soon. I am so deeply hurt that I did not feel I could present these things to you personally without breaking down, so I am writing this letter instead."

But there were others who had been listening to the sermons and examining their consciences, and they had concluded that bigotry had no place in Christianity. They were supportive all summer.

So were people from other churches in the community. "We wish Catholics could vote," a Catholic friend told Daddy. Some in the community viewed the vote as a purely personal thing. They liked my father, and they hated for anything bad to happen to him. Others saw the vote as more than a referendum on whether he stayed or was forced to leave. They saw it as a vote on the future of the town.

When the night finally came, the church was packed. We watched from the parsonage next door as people filed in. Daddy paced the floor. I smoked a cigarette and he bummed one from me, the only time that ever happened.

Dad presided over the meeting as prescribed in the church bylaws. The first issue was whether the vote would be by secret ballot or by standing vote. The opponents wanted a secret ballot, believing that more people would be likely to vote their prejudices if they didn't have to do it in public. But after some debate, the church voted to have a standing vote in keeping with church procedure. At that point, we were fairly certain we had won.

Before the actual vote, Daddy called on the school principal for prayer. I don't recall the words of his prayer, but I remember that it called for reason and wisdom and love and set the tone for the vote to follow.

Then we voted. Those in favor of my dad staying were asked to stand. Two-thirds of the congregation jumped to their feet. Then those opposed were asked to stand. Less than a third voted to fire him. A few of the opponents, seeing that they had lost, didn't vote. The verdict was an overwhelming vote of confidence, not just for my dad but for the message he had proclaimed.

The ordeal our family went through that summer could have turned me off Christianity. But it had exactly the opposite effect. I had watched a man stand up for what he believed, do what he knew to be right, and put his faith on the line. That was a religious experience, a turning point in my own faith.

My father continued to preach at that church in that little Texas town until he retired. He approached the end of his life with the quiet satisfaction that it had counted for something. He had a positive and profound impact on his community. He did his part to make this a little better world than he found it. He kept the faith.

All that should be enough for any of us, but there is one thing more. That summer long ago, my dad became my hero.

A Strong, Kind Woman

My mother was smart, brave, humble and kind. Most of all, kind.

Maybe we all grow up thinking our own mother is the closest thing to perfection we'll know. At least I hope that's how you feel.

I did. And she was.

She grew up on a farm, the second of five children, all girls but the last, who naturally gained the nickname Boy. Her parents believed strongly in education, her own mother being a former teacher. All the children finished high school, three went on to college, despite the Depression, despite the fact that her father went blind and couldn't farm anymore.

In the '30s she taught in her hometown of Pearsall, Texas, teaching Hispanic children to read, write and speak English.

Mother, second from left, with her sisters, Cile, Gladys and Irma.

Later she campaigned for, and was elected, county school superintendent.

A young preacher from San Antonio, six years younger than she, came to the little church her family attended, and the woman who would become my mother gave up her political career to become a preacher's wife.

It wasn't easy being a preacher's wife and a mother. We never had enough money, although that seemed to worry my father more than it did my mother.

It didn't bother her to be in the background while Daddy was in the spotlight. I suppose that's because she had an

My mother, Minnie Lee Sharber, as a college student.

inner strength, a healthy sense of who she was, which enabled her to put others first and herself second.

Those who knew her felt that strength. She was the person—in the town, in the church, in the family—who got things done. If she saw a need, she knew what to do about it, quietly, without fanfare or recognition.

She took meals to the sick. She counseled young people about their careers, their education, their faith. She befriended young families who were just getting started and old people who needed special attention. She taught English to migrant workers.

Mother was not afraid to tackle new challenges. In 1960 she organized and supervised the taking of the census in our county. One year she ran the local office for a statewide political candidate. For several years she was an employment counselor for the state employment office. After work, at home, she would sometimes make calls on her own trying to help people find jobs.

One year she substituted for a teacher who had to go to a sanitarium with tuberculosis. Years later I learned that she taught the whole time for no pay, insisting that her paycheck be sent to the man's family.

She especially enjoyed hosting receptions and cooking church suppers. Cooking was her avocation, her great love.

She didn't think of it as a chore but as a release. She could lose herself in the kitchen. She clipped recipes with a passion and was always trying out some new concoction on us. People loved to come to dinner at our house, but it wasn't until I was grown and away from home that I truly appreciated how great a cook she was.

I didn't know until I was almost grown that Mother nearly died after my younger brother Charlie was born. She had Addison's Disease, which was fairly rare and nearly always fatal back in the '50s. When the doctors diagnosed her illness after months of tests, she was given a pamphlet to read. In short, it said, she didn't have long to live.

She grew weaker and weaker. Sometimes, she said, she would get exhausted just from turning over in bed. She worried about dying, not because she feared it, but because she hated to leave her husband to raise two young boys alone.

Then came Cortisone. The drug saved her life. And for almost twenty-five years she lived a normal life, despite the disease. Finally, in 1976, when she was sixty-three, complications from the disease took her life.

In her final weeks, she invited her two granddaughters to come for what she knew would be a last visit. She was sicker than any of us realized, and she was afraid that if we knew how bad she was we wouldn't let the girls stay. So she pretended to be fine until we had left. She told a friend that she was determined to have that time with those children, and no one was going to deny her that pleasure.

Even as she lay dying in the hospital, in great pain, her last thoughts were of others. She called a young girl to offer her some advice. She had her brother-in-law bring a cake to her hospital room so she could throw one last party—for the nurses who had cared for her. The next night she died.

In my family—and I suspect in most families—we prayed to God as "our Heavenly Father," and we thought of God in masculine terms. But over the years, I have come to believe that God has a feminine quality as well. In my mother, I saw the pure love of God in the living flesh.

Daddy preached it. Mother exuded it.

Whatever Happened to the Extended Family?

On my mother's side of the family, my great-great-grand-parents, my great-grandparents and my grandparents all lived within a few miles of each other all their lives. Their children grew up in the same area and most stayed right there.

To a large extent our family is something of a microcosm of what has happened in America.

The family's roots were rural. They were all farmers until the Depression, until my grandfather lost his eyesight, until World War II came along. Everything began to change.

My mother moved with my father to his new job in a small town nearly three hundred miles away. It must have seemed to the family—a family that for generations had all lived no more than a day's buggy ride apart—that she had moved to the other side of the world.

One of her sisters took a job in the big city sixty miles from the farm. Another sister moved with her husband to a town two hundred miles away. One sister and a brother stayed nearby, close to the land. They would all get back together a couple of times a year, but the migration had begun, just like it had all over America.

My generation was extremely mobile. We went to college. We moved where the good jobs were, mostly in cities, often hundreds of miles from family.

We had children, and they grew up not even as close to grandparents and aunts and uncles and cousins as we were. A few stayed close to the farm, but most headed off on their own, again going where the jobs were, where the opportunities were, where the money was, to the cities, in some cases even to other states.

My daughters grew up in Texas. Today one lives in New York; the other has moved to another country because of her husband's job.

The extended family is not as close as the family I knew growing up. There have been several divorces, a few deaths. We've become preoccupied with our own lives, our careers, our immediate families.

Most of us still live in Texas, and a few remain within fifty miles of the old family farm. We still try to get together every year or two, although it seems to be increasingly difficult to do so. Except for funerals. Then we head back home from wherever we are, as many as can, regretting that we haven't been closer and promising to stay in touch with each other from now on.

Technology, particularly the automobile, fed the mobility that broke up the extended family. But it may well be technology that keeps families together in the future.

Today's extended families are already using the computer to bridge the physical distances that separate us, linking us to each other through e-mail, web sites, and cell phones. It may not be quite the same as having grandma just down the road, but families have always had to cope with change. This time the change promises to draw us closer, if not in person then at least in spirit.

Mammaw and Dang-Dang

My grandfather was blind. He went blind as an adult, and he had to give up farming. But he never gave up the farm. He and my grandmother continued to live there until they died, and the farm still remains in the family. I try to go there every year or so because the place has such a warm spot in my memory.

The place and the people. Mostly the people.

I was blessed to have grandparents who not only loved me but liked me. They seemed to be glad when I was around.

My grandfather and I would lie in bed and listen to San Antonio Missions Texas League baseball games until we went to sleep. He liked for me to join him in listening to his "talking books," recorded especially for the blind on long-playing records, long before the advent of "books on tape." I usually went to sleep listening to them, too.

Dang-Dang, in the dark glasses, and Mammaw, far right, with several of their grandchildren. Dang-Dang went blind at about age 40.

He could read Braille and had a Braille typewriter, which he didn't really use very much. He would give us grandkids his Braille books when he was finished with them. They were great for Show and Tell, and I still have one to remember him by.

We thought it was real grown-up to pretend we were blind. We would close our eyes and take his cane and walk around bumping into chairs and walls. We meant no disrespect. In fact, we thought he was very special.

And he was. Every Christmas he gave each grandkid a silver dollar. I saved them all until I was eighteen or so, then cashed them in somewhere along the way. I wish I had kept them.

Because he lived out in the country, he had to walk a mile to get the mail. When I was visiting, I never missed going with him. It was the best part of the day, just the two of us walking down the dirt road, me asking questions and him patiently answering them.

He died walking home from that mail box. I was sixteen, and I still remember my mother's face when she came to get me out of football practice to tell me Dang-Dang was dead.

What funny names we sometimes give our grandparents. Dang-Dang and Mammaw were so named by an older cousin, but the rest of us never questioned the names. So Dang-Dang and Mammaw it was.

Mammaw was a fiery competitor. We would stay up all night playing card and board games. No matter what the game, she played to win. None of this "let the grandson win"

Mammaw on her 80th birthday.

stuff for her. If I was old enough to play, then I was old enough to beat.

I'm sure she actually threw a few games my way, but she would always carry on as if she had lost the World Series if I beat her in a game of gin rummy or dominoes or Sorry.

She was a lot of fun. When she would visit us in the fall, she liked to gather pecans from our yard. But she was impatient. If all the pecans hadn't fallen by the time she was ready to harvest them, she would have us throw our football at them to knock them out of the tree.

Once, when we were at school, she enlisted the help of some man who just happened to be walking by. There they were, an old woman and a stranger, throwing a football up in a pecan tree.

Everybody ought to have—or be—grandparents like that.

Christmas in the Country

Christmas memories are made of these:

The endless drive to grandmother's house...Seeing the Christmas lights in small town after small town along the way... Christmas carols playing softly on the car radio and wishing for some rock'n'roll...Sleeping on the back seat and trying to convince my little brother to take the floorboard...Asking for the hundredth time, "How many more miles?"

Finally, the feeling as the car turns off pavement onto the gravel country road...Honking the horn as we come up the lane...Being greeted enthusiastically by aunts and uncles and cousins...The warm feeling of belonging.

The freedom of being in the country...Hunting rabbits with a .410 shotgun... Pretending to like the taste and texture of fried jackrabbit.

Gathering eggs at Mammaw's hen house.

Having to go to the outhouse in the middle of the night...Saturday night baths in a wash-tub...Peaceful, restful, but never boring, lazy days...The adults setting off Roman candles while we kids light sparklers.

The smell of turkey cooking on Christmas morning... Great country vegetables...All the cousins eating off card tables while the big folks get the dining table...The day when you're not a kid anymore and get to join the adults...Wondering why anyone would eat mincemeat pie when there are so many delicious desserts available.

Sleeping on a screened porch in the winter under several pounds of quilts...Waking up to a cold house...Backing up to a wood stove.

Eating all the peppermint sticks you want...Singing hymns around an out-of-tune piano...Sitting in my grandfather's lap...Staying up late to play dominoes or cards with a grandmother who loved competition and grandchildren, maybe in that order...Spending hours working a jigsaw puzzle...Snuggling up next to grandfather in bed...Walking a mile with him to get the mail.

Carrying buckets of rain water from the cistern to the house...Chopping wood and not being very good at it...Feeding the chickens corn...Helping grandfather milk the cows… Watching grandmother churn butter…Thinking that all the work around a farm was a lot like playing—when there are plenty of cousins around.

Eating divinity, and understanding how it got its name…Wondering why the adults sort of giggled when they talked about drinking eggnog…Learning why…Having fried quail for dinner one night during the holidays and liking that much better than jackrabbit.

Wishing the holidays would never end.

The First Time
I Saw Santa

Can you remember the first time you saw Santa Claus? I do. Well, not the first time I looked at Santa or sat in Santa's lap or gazed into Santa's beard. I don't remember those.

But I do remember the first time I really *saw* Santa.

I'm not sure how old I was, probably six or seven, and I'm fairly sure at the time I didn't realize what I had seen. I do remember it was a Christmas Eve, and it was after dark. We were in a hurry to leave town and drive to my grandparents' farm house where there would be cousins to play with, good things to eat, and plenty of presents.

We usually didn't leave for their house until after noon on Christmas Eve, frequently not until after dark. That time it wasn't until after dark.

My dad had been working all day—probably with Billy Bryant and Annie Mae Hardage—helping deliver baskets of food and toys to the needy families in our community. That day, as I remember it, all the deliveries had been made but one.

There was a house a couple of miles outside of town where a struggling young couple lived with their children— I'm not sure how many.

Daddy said he would deliver the food and toys to that home before we headed out of town. We stopped outside the shack where the family lived. We waited in the car while dad went inside.

For some reason he decided to put on a Santa suit he had used earlier in the Christmas season—at the church Christmas program or as the town's Santa arriving on the fire truck. He was wearing the Santa suit as he stepped out of the car and started making his way to the shanty.

As he approached the house, the children—who no doubt had been told by their parents not to expect anything for Christmas that year—saw him coming.

They began to jump and shout for joy. Santa was at the doorstep. And he had presents for *them*. Santa had not forgotten.

"I told you he would come!" the oldest brother shrieked. "I told you he would come!"

That was the first time I saw Santa.

Democrats on TV

One of the first shows I remember watching on TV was the Democratic National Convention.

Daddy bought our first TV in August 1956, just a week or so before my twelfth birthday and a few days before the Democratic convention. I knew the TV wasn't for my birthday.

We were excited to have a TV finally, even though with rabbit ears we could only get one station. Still, it carried "Gunsmoke" and "Have Gun Will Travel" – and, of course, the Democratic National Convention. And we watched it, by golly, until the screen went fuzzy.

Two things I remember from that convention: (1) the keynote address was by the governor of Tennessee, whose last name was Clement, the same as my great-grandmother, and my dad claimed his grandfather's family had come from Tennessee, so we were bound to be related; and (2) the nomination of Sen. Estes Kefauver for vice president.

Funny, but I don't recall a thing about Adlai Stevenson's nomination or his speech or anything else except that he threw open the nomination for vice president to the delegates. It came down to Senator Kefauver from Tennessee and a young senator from Massachusetts by the name of Kennedy. I didn't know a thing about either one, but since Kefauver was from the South, I rooted for him. He won, but it was pretty close, if my memory serves.

By the 1960 Democratic National Convention, we still had the same black-and-white TV, but we no longer watched it every night until the screen went fuzzy. However, we still watched the Democrats.

That young senator from Massachusetts was back, this time as the favorite for the presidential nomination. But, of course, we were for the Texas senator, Lyndon Johnson. Not only was Johnson from Texas, but Kennedy was—we lowered our voices when we dared say it—a Catholic.

Daddy was a Baptist preacher and loved everyone, but his understanding of ecuminism hadn't yet extended to the possibility of a Catholic in the White House. Not as long as they had a Pope who would almost certainly tell an American president what to do.

We suffered through Kennedy's nomination. Even though we were cheered somewhat when Johnson was selected as the running mate, I remember it being a fairly gloomy period in our family. A Catholic as president? It was just a matter of time until Baptists were persecuted in the street.

Perhaps I remember it being worse than it really was. Memories do play tricks. But that's how I remember it nonetheless. Though the whole thing sounds ridiculous now, back then it seemed awfully serious around our house.

My father was among the Baptist ministers who heard Kennedy address the religious issue in Houston, and he came back less worried about a papal dictatorship. My folks were smiling again.

A week or so before the election, I asked Mother whom they would be voting for. "Kennedy and Johnson," she said, rationalizing that "God will probably be more likely to forgive us for voting for a Catholic than for a Republican." Democratic roots ran deep in my family.

Daddy remained a loyal Democrat all his life, even when many Texas Democrats switched allegiance, especially after the chaotic 1968 convention and the nomination of George

McGovern in 1972. Dad was a McGovern delegate to the county convention.

Even when I would suggest in later years that a particular Democratic candidate for state office might be considerably less worthy than his Republican opponent, Daddy remained a straight-ticket voter.

Texas has changed during my lifetime from a two party state—conservative Democrats and liberal Democrats—to a state controlled by and large by Republicans. That was unthinkable in Texas in the '50s, even though the state went for Eisenhower over Stevenson.

Over the years, I've become something of a political independent, voting more for the candidate than for the party. But, I have to admit, when it comes to watching the conventions on TV, I still prefer the show the Democrats put on.

When Kennedy Died

If you were old enough to be aware, it's a moment that is locked into your memory. A frozen segment of time.

Where were you when you heard President Kennedy had been shot?

People who were in at least junior high school remember the scene like it was yesterday. A friend said he was playing table tennis at his college when the announcement came over the loud speaker. Suddenly there was absolute silence in the student center. Another friend, who was in sixth grade, remembers praying to God to save the president's life. My brother's seventh-grade basketball team was about to take the court when the coach called them together and, with tears streaming down his cheeks, told them the president had died. A woman friend recalled she was fixing lunch for her son when the news came on the TV. She burst into tears.

I was a sophomore in college and had just finished waiting tables in the dining hall. I was walking back to my dorm when a student I worked with on the student newspaper ran by and yelled that Kennedy and Johnson had been shot.

"Yeah, sure," I replied.

"Well, I'm going to watch it on TV," he yelled back as he ran on.

I was with another waiter. We walked on a few seconds wondering if the messenger had been telling the truth. Surely not. That couldn't happen in America. Not in Texas. Then we too started running for the dorm.

We listened in shock to the reports on the radio confirming that the president and Governor Connally, not Vice President Johnson, had been shot in Dallas. I don't recall that I cried, but I was stunned. I just kept sitting there listening to the radio, even after the somber news that the president had died.

Finally, it occurred to me that maybe I should go over to the student newspaper office and see if my help was needed. But our editor had already stopped the presses for that day's edition and printed out a new front page with the news of the assassination.

Life as we knew it was put on hold. Classes were canceled. A memorial service was held on campus. Many students went home for the weekend. Most at least called home. Everyone was glued to the television.

For today's generation, the terrorist attack on New York and Washington on September 11, 2001, was the cataclysmic event of this era, just as the attack on Pearl Harbor on December 7, 1941, was the defining moment of that era.

For my generation, no other single event made such an impression as the assassination of President Kennedy on November 22, 1963—a day that changed our country, our world, our lives. A day we will never forget.

Collapse of Communism

I don't remember being all that scared about the scourge of communism or the threat of nuclear annihilation. In our town we didn't go through the school drills I've seen in photos, where everyone would hide under their desks in case of nuclear attack, as if that would help. If there were fallout shelters in our town, I was unaware of them.

Perhaps I was just too young to be worried about such things. Or maybe it was because my parents had a deep and optimistic faith. But for whatever reason, I grew up in the '50s a lot more concerned about the outcome of the Yankees vs. Dodgers in the World Series than the prospect of America going communist or being blitzed into oblivion.

There was a teacher in high school who professed membership in, or an affinity for, the super-right John Birch

Society. As part of our American history class, we had to write and present papers on communism and the John Birch movement. We were free, he said, to take whatever stand we could defend.

No doubt influenced by my father's optimistic liberalism and unwavering faith in the future, I chose to criticize the John Birchers and others on the right who were casting suspicion on everyone in government who was to the left of center. Although the history teacher—who had engaged in long, spirited, but friendly discussions with my father—did not agree with my thesis, he awarded me an A nevertheless.

Somehow I always figured that the good guys would win. Communism didn't make economic sense, at least not in a country with a strong middle class, because it limited the possibilities for economic advancement. Most of us would never be rich, but we wanted to hold to the slim chance, the dream, that we might hit it big.

And then there was the matter of political freedom— speech, dissent, press, religion, open elections. Communist regimes, like other dictatorships, inevitably cracked down on people's rights to express themselves, to disagree, to oppose the established leadership. Communism couldn't flourish in an open society, and America has long been the most open society in the world.

So I wasn't worried too much about America going communist. I have always thought a greater danger at home lay in a tendency by some to stifle dissent and cast suspicion and aspersions on their fellow Americans.

Nor was I too surprised to see communism collapse in Russia and begin its worldwide decline. I visited Russia in 1991, just weeks before communism's official demise. I saw a country in economic chaos, the country's resources drained from having to support a costly military and political machine for decades.

Things just didn't seem to work well. Food lines were long. Stores were empty. Buildings were drab. Medicine was scarce. Cars broke down and were abandoned on the side of the road. The cost of living was skyrocketing, the value of the ruble plummeting. Wages were pathetic.

The old guard communists blamed the problems on the new regime and called for restoring order through military control. But those efforts, fortunately, failed to materialize. The Russian people had gone that route for nearly three-quarters of a century by then, and clearly it had not worked.

I have to think that much of the credit for the demise of communism should be given to American television. As much as we might criticize the effects of TV on our culture, TV has shown people throughout the world what they are missing, how the other half lives.

The longest lines in Russia when I visited there were not the bread lines. They were the lines that stretched for blocks of whole families waiting to get into Moscow's only McDonald's.

The Queen & I

Like most kids, I grew up reading about kings and queens and magical kingdoms. Like most kids, I figured those were just fairy tales.

The best-known king or queen in my lifetime has been Queen Elizabeth II. She was crowned queen in 1952, when I was just eight, and she has been queen ever since.

One day, when I was much older, I received an embossed invitation in the mail. It read:

"On the occasion of the Visit of Her Majesty Queen Elizabeth II and His Royal Highness The Prince Philip, Duke of Edinburgh, The British Ambassador is commanded by The Queen to invite Glenn Dromgoole to a Reception at the Four Seasons Hotel, Austin, on Monday, 20th May, 1991, at 2:30 p.m."

The British Ambassador was *commanded* to invite me to this reception. I quickly accepted, before The Queen had time to change her mind.

Now, of course, I knew this wasn't a private one-on-one reception. I wasn't about to become a Knight or anything. And I did wonder how I made the list. After all, The Queen and I had not been all that close. Why me? Why had The Queen commanded the British Ambassador to invite me to a reception?

So I called the British Ambassador to find out. I figured the Ambassador would say, "Glenn Who?" But he didn't. In fact, I didn't talk to him at all. But I did talk to Linda Kelly in the British Consulate-General's office in Houston. She was real nice. She knew who I was and why I was invited. It turns out I would be one of a hundred and twenty-five "working journalists" at the reception, and each of us would be presented to The Queen. I was put on the list by the governor's office.

"Uh, what does one do when one is presented to The Queen?" I asked Miss Kelly.

"You may bow if you wish or shake her hand," she replied in her delightful British accent.

"How does one address The Queen?" I asked.

"You may call her Your Majesty on first reference, if you wish. After that, you may call her Mom," she said.

"Mom?" I thought. "I may call The Queen of England Mom?"

Then I realized that what Miss Kelly really was saying was that I could call her "Ma'am." In British, "Ma'am" sounds like "Mom." Strange language, British.

And let's not forget His Royal Highness The Prince Philip, Duke of Edinburgh. According to protocol, I could refer to him as "Your Royal Highness" on first reference and as "Sir" thereafter. (Not "Dad?")

A colleague gave me a list of Things Not to Do and Things Not to Say When Meeting Queen Elizabeth (Mom). "Don't tell her that you always loved 'Queen for a Day' when it was on TV," he advised. "Don't remind her that the Colonists whupped Britain's butt in 1776. Don't say, 'Of course, y'all know that Elvis is still the King.' "

When I arrived at the Four Seasons Hotel with the other hundred or so "working journalists," we were served drinks and hors d'oeuvres (or snaaacks, as we would say in Texan). The snaaacks weren't your usual chips and salsa either. We had lobster, crab, swordfish and other stuff too exotic to name. Most of it was pretty tasty, except for the pheasant mousse on blueberry bread. I suppose it's an acquired taste.

When The Queen arrived, she and Prince Philip and two other British officials formed a receiving line outside the ballroom. As each of us approached The Queen, we handed a name card to a press spokesman, who turned and announced us to Her Majesty.

The line moved quickly. All we had time to do was say "Pleased to meet you" or "How do you do" or "Welcome to Texas," something like that. She extended her gloved hand, and we shook hands. Then we shook hands with His Royal Highness. Some of us nodded, but I didn't see anyone bow. A couple of female Texas journalists, former British subjects, curtsied.

After everyone had gone through the line, The Queen and Prince Philip mingled with the reporters for half an hour or more. It appeared to me that anyone who wanted to speak privately for a few moments with The Queen had the opportunity.

I asked a fellow editor if he had been able to speak to The Queen. "A word's worth," he replied.

The reception was entirely off the record, which means we couldn't report anything that was said. But I don't think it would be breaking the rules of confidentiality to tell you that both Her Majesty and His Royal Highness (Mom and Sir) were very pleasant and cordial and patient.

It must be tedious to chitchat with people you've never seen before, will never see again, and who have very little to do with anything of significance to you. But they tolerated it well.

As you've probably observed from photos of the Royal Couple, they don't dress all that royally. No capes or crowns or anything like that. Prince Philip wore a gray business suit, and The Queen wore a floral print dress and a yellow hat.

These days, I suppose, it's a bit of an anachronism to have a Royal Family, and a rather expensive one at that. But as one journalist at the reception put it, "This is the first time my mother has been the least bit interested in anything I've done."

In the storybooks, kings and queens were always associated with living happily ever after. Somehow, in these days of logic and practicality and cold reality, a little of that magic lives on. A boy from Sour Lake, Texas, grows up and gets to meet the Queen of England. That's magical enough for me.

Six Men

We never used the word mentor, of course. Not back then. But through the years, if we are lucky, people come into our lives and influence us in positive ways.

Whether we call them mentors or teachers, or just friends, they are the adults who have a lasting influence on us. Too often we neglect to take the time to let them know what they have meant to us, how much we appreciate the time and attention they gave us.

These six men, I now realize, were my mentors. Perhaps they will remind you of yours.

I. First Male Teacher

He was my first male teacher and the first teacher who treated me like a young man instead of a little kid. His name was Mr. Watson. Well, Mister wasn't his first name. But that was the name we called him, you can be sure. Officially, he was Joe Watson. To us, he was Mr. Watson.

We had him in the fifth grade. Most of the kids wanted Mrs. Sexton. She was nice. Mr. Watson's reputation was that he was tough. Mrs. Sexton was a Sunday school teacher in our Baptist church, and I figured if I got her, my dad being the Baptist pastor, fifth grade would be a breeze.

I didn't get her. I got Mr. Watson. I'm glad I did.

Besides helping me grow up, Mr. Watson helped me learn to do math quickly. He taught us. He encouraged us. He pushed us.

We had daily contests to see who could work math problems on the chalkboard the fastest. He made us think on our feet. When we competed against Mrs. Sexton's class, we always won. And I turned out to be the fastest of the fast.

Never before in my young life had I been The Star of the team. But when it came to math on the chalkboard, I was. Whatever the problem, be it long division or addition or multiplication, I could do it faster than anyone else. Mr. Watson recognized that potential, cultivated it, brought it out.

At recess, Mr. Watson pitched for our continuing softball game between his class and Mrs. Sexton's class. Each game started on Monday and continued through Friday. I don't remember who won those games, but I remember that Mr. Watson always cheered for us when we made a good play in the field or managed to get a hit off his pitching.

I came away from fifth grade with three lasting impressions:

1. Math is important in life.

2. Baseball is a great game.

3. We ought to have more men teachers.

II. The One-Armed Coach

My first coach had one strong arm and one big heart.

Coach McCarson was the coach for the whole town back then. He was the high school football coach, but he also coached basketball and Little League baseball. I had him in Little League.

The fact that he had one arm couldn't be ignored. He had lost the arm in a childhood accident. But no one would have thought to suggest that Coach McCarson was handicapped in any way. He had compensated by building up that arm until he was stronger than most men with two arms. Today we might call it a bionic arm.

Coach could hit a ball farther than anyone I've seen before or since. He would stand at home plate, hold the bat in his one hand, and hit fly balls that would seem to go into orbit. During church league softball games, his team always won because he was by far the fastest pitcher and the best hitter in town.

Above all, he was a good man. He was kind and gentle with us, even when we messed up, which as Little Leaguers was fairly often. I remember one game at second base when I dropped two pop-ups in the same inning with the bases loaded. After the inning, he simply told me to try to relax out there.

I played second base because Coach kept trying me at different positions until he found one that I, a skinny kid with a weak arm, could handle. He made a special effort to see that I had an opportunity to play. And he did the same with all the boys.

I had to miss part of one season because of illness. But as soon as I was able to play, he found a way to get me in the game for a couple of innings. Usually, I split time at second base with Leland Ray, who was a better athlete. One game Leland would play the first three innings and I would play the last three; the next game I would start and he would finish. Coach McCarson understood that everyone needed an opportunity to play.

One time we ran up the score on an opposing team, beating them 51-1 and scoring 32 runs in the second inning. But Coach wasn't trying to run up the score. He played everyone we had, but there was just no accounting for the ineptness of the other team. If he could have, I'm sure he would have gladly switched places with the other team's coach.

Unfortunately, the high school football team didn't win enough games, and that was what really counted with the school board—not the Little League coaching or the fact that he was the dominant pitcher and hitter in the church softball league and an active member of the church he actually played for.

The year after I finished Little League, he was fired. He left our town, got out of coaching, and operated his own service station for a number of years in a nearby city. Through hard work, honesty, personality and service, he built the station into the best in the city.

He was a man of strength, dignity, integrity, compassion and pride, and he had a profound influence on the young lives he touched.

III. Talking Baseball

When you're growing up, it helps to have some adults you can talk to. Besides your parents, of course.

For me, the adult was Mr. Carney. His friends called him Arthur, but I never felt comfortable calling him that—even later when I was grown. To me he was always Mr. Carney.

Mr. Carney and I had one thing in common. We both lived, loved, talked, breathed baseball.

I was fourteen or so, about the age when I probably should have begun taking an interest in girls. But I hadn't—yet. I still rode a bike, still carried my baseball glove, still thought I might get my shot at the Majors.

Mr. Carney, of course, knew better, though he said nothing to burst my bubble.

Unlike me, Mr. Carney actually had a legitimate shot at a professional baseball career. But a war and an injury had cut short his dream. When I knew him, he was in his late thirties, I assume, about the age of my father. He was coaching a Little League team. I was past my prime, athletically, at fourteen but didn't know it.

One day, having been passed over for a Pony League try-out, I was watching Mr. Carney's Little League team practice. He asked me why I wasn't at Pony League practice. I told him I hadn't been asked to try out.

"Well, why don't you help us?" he said. So I did. I became an assistant coach with the Yankees. We won the league a couple of times, which didn't have much to do with me, but Mr. Carney and his assistant, Mr. Johnston, made me feel like I was a vital part of the coaching staff.

Mostly, Mr. Carney made me feel accepted by a grownup. He was my first male adult friend. In the summer, when he would get off work in the oil fields, I would be there to welcome him home. He would sit and drink coffee with his wife, and I would hang on his every word.

When we talked baseball, we talked as peers. We would discuss the strategy for our next game, and how that might affect the strategy for the game after that.

Maybe he got as much out of it as I did. Maybe he liked being looked up to, being a role model. All I know is that when I was with Mr. Carney, I felt more responsible, more mature, more complete. He treated me like an equal. He made me feel important. He made me a full partner, not only in his team but in his life.

IV. FIRST PRESS CARD

The first newspaper editor I ever knew wasn't much of an editor at all. He almost never covered news or wrote editorials. Basically what he did was run a print shop. He took whatever news or ads people brought in, typed them on his

Linotype machine, and printed them in his paper. He wasn't exactly what you would call a mentor. But he played an important, maybe even crucial role, in my decision to become a journalist.

You see, he gave me a chance. He gave me time. He gave me space. He gave me encouragement. And he gave me my first press card.

I was still in junior high when I began "covering" sports for his newspaper. My first articles were about Little League baseball. Pretty soon I was writing up the high school football and basketball games, mainly because no one else was doing it and it seemed that someone should.

Whatever I took in, he printed. And whatever sports I covered were the only sports articles in the paper. So pretty soon I declared myself Sports Editor. Which was fine with him since it was cheaper than paying me anything.

One day I decided the Sports Editor should cover a college football game. Mainly I just wanted to go to the game and get in free. So he hand-set some type and printed me a press card identifying me as a representative of the newspaper, entitled to whatever courtesies and privileges were accorded the press.

It worked. For years the press card got me into games, most of which I actually wrote about. I continued to write a sports column for the paper, always for free, even after I went off to college. But in college I discovered Editorials and other Important Things and started writing about them.

The editor and I remained friends, and after I landed my first real newspaper job I would always drop by to talk shop with him when I was home. He continued to take an interest in me and my career until the day he died.

And I still have that first press card, framed, signed by B.L. Cornwell, Editor, the *Oil City Visitor*.

V. Favorite Professor

David Bowers became my mentor when I was twenty, and he would fill that role for thirty-five years. I don't think I ever told him he was my mentor, but I'm sure he knew it.

David—or Dr. Bowers, as I called him back then—came to teach journalism at our college my junior year. The first time I met him was at registration. When I checked my class schedule, I found that I had "Bowers" for four classes. I figured I had better meet him.

I found him working the registration table for the journalism department. I introduced myself and mentioned that I would have him for four classes that fall.

"We're going to need to get along," I joked.

"One of us is," he shot back.

Well, we did. His door was literally always open to me, and I often stopped by to seek his advice when I was managing editor, then editor of the student newspaper. We were undergoing censorship battles with the administration, and David's was always a voice of common sense, moderation, reason and encouragement. Above all, encouragement.

I respected him from the moment I met him because of his background as a newspaper editor before he became a professor. He peppered his lectures with real-life examples from his own experience. He authored his own editing workbook and filled it with grammatical challenges he had encountered on the newspapers he had edited. He offered advice based on what had worked for him—and hadn't worked—in daily newspaper management.

He introduced me to the writing of William Allen White, the Kansas editor who died the year I was born and who would become something of a role model for my own career as an editor. (White's editorials "What's the Matter with Kansas?" and "Mary White" are two of the greatest newspaper editorials in American history.)

He hammered home the importance of a clear, concise lead—or first paragraph—of a story. If you don't capture the reader's attention in the first paragraph, he stressed, it doesn't really matter what else you write. If you have an hour to write a story, he would say, spend fifty minutes on the lead—that's how important it is.

Don't waste words, he challenged. Don't waste the reader's time with unnecessary verbiage, long sentences, cumbersome paragraphs. In newspapers, space is money, and words fill space. Make every word count for something.

He taught me to communicate passion in editorials and to give leadership to the community the newspaper served—to see the editorial page as the *soul* of the newspaper.

But beyond all that, as every good teacher should, he inspired me and uplifted me and caused me to want to be better. He raised my standards. He raised my expectations. He raised my vision.

His teaching lasted well beyond the two years I studied under him. Throughout my career, I always knew I could call on David for good advice. By then, he was David, not Dr. Bowers, and he was my friend, not my professor. But he never ceased being my teacher, or my mentor.

VI. Shades of Gray

One of the finest newspapermen—one of the finest *men*—I have known was Jack Butler.

Mr. Butler was editor of the *Fort Worth Star-Telegram* during those troubling years of the '60s and early '70s. He played a critical role in keeping Fort Worth relatively calm while many other cities were experiencing great turmoil.

In virtually everything he did, Mr. Butler—I never did feel comfortable calling him Jack, even after we had worked together for fourteen years—urged reason and fairness. The minister at his funeral couldn't have selected a more appropriate verse than Micah 6:8: "And what does the Lord require of you but to do justice, and to love kindness, and to walk humbly with your God?"

For three years I had the privilege of serving on the newspaper's editorial page staff. Each morning at nine-thirty the five or six of us would gather in Mr. Butler's spacious office, pour ourselves some coffee, and discuss the events of the day. It was a learning and maturing process for me, and I look back fondly on those years. I brought very little to the party other than an empty cup, into which would be poured much more than coffee.

I came to see that issues are rarely black and white but varying shades of gray. I became more appreciative of a newspaper's role in helping to influence the character of a community. I started to understand the importance of incremental progress, of taking one small step here and another there, instead of great leaps.

Mr. Butler taught us to keep things in perspective, to laugh at ourselves, to be charitable toward others whose motives we could not know in full. He showed us that usually we could accomplish more by gently nudging than by raking someone over the coals.

Mostly, I remember a man who took a great deal of pleasure in what he did. He enjoyed being a newspaper editor. He thought it was important work. And he also laughed a lot.

I have saved a letter from him for thirty years. I was on a study leave from the paper at the time. He had written to me in response to a letter in which I must have raised some dark philosophical questions.

"Did you ever consider," he wrote, "that your inability to accept extremes in philosophy might just make you an intellectually discriminating moderate? It has been my observation that as I have matured, I have found all the deep shades of opinion were invalid. There are almost always some valid points in either persuasion.

"It seems to me," he continued, "that I come down more and more in the position that most of us—at any given time—do the best we can under the circumstances at hand.

"Mary Lou [his wife] often raises philosophical debates about how well we did with our children. She wishes we had done this or that differently. But looking back I say to myself, 'Yeah, sure, I did that badly.' But I did not ever do it badly because I meant to do it badly. Given my economic position, my state of exhaustion, my incomplete knowledge, my sense of insecurity—at any given moment I did the best I could."

And, then, as was typical, he laughed in closing: "This will teach you to write philosophical notes to me."

Indeed it did. I just wish I had written more of them.

I Want to Speak to a Live Human Being!

Around our house we have two portable telephones, one phone with an answering machine and fax, three cell phones, caller ID, call waiting, and three-way calling.

I have to marvel at how far telephones have come in my lifetime. I can remember when we didn't even have dial phones. In our town if you needed to make a call, you picked up the receiver and asked the operator to connect you.

I was very small then, but I distinctly recall picking up the receiver and telling the operator, "I need to talk to my daddy," and she would ring his office.

When we got dial phone service and essentially did away with local operators, the phone company had a big reception to show off its new facility, which was little more than a small room full of wires and switches.

Dial service brought new phone numbers for everyone in town and a prefix that we really didn't have to use as long as we were calling another number in town. The prefix for our town was Atlas—AT being the only part of the word that mattered. Our phone number at the parsonage was AT7-3720. My dad's study at the church was AT7-3427. More than forty years later, those were still the numbers for the parsonage and the church, except the AT had been replaced by the numerical 28, which is the same thing. I saw a woman a few years ago whom I hadn't seen in years, and I could still remember Mrs. Richey's phone number. It was, and remained, just one digit off from the church's number.

After dial service came to town, nearly everyone had private phone lines. No more *party lines,* where two or more homes had to share the same line. My grandmother was on a party line out in the country, and often when we would pick up the phone at her house to make a call, someone else would be talking on it. We would have to wait until they were through before we could use the phone. When the phone rang, we didn't pick it up unless it was her code—four long rings.

Today many families have at least two private lines in their home—one for the adults and one for the kids—especially if there are teen-agers in the house. Imagine the frustration of having to share a party line with a home that had a teen-ager. When I was a teen-ager, I was either talking on the phone or wishing it would ring. That's one thing about phones that hasn't changed.

But there is a huge downside to all this telephone technology, and it has to do with personal customer service. We've gone from a local operator saying "Number, please" to recordings designed to make it virtually impossible to ever talk to a live person.

I called the phone company not long ago. I wanted to add a service, one of those machines that can tell you who's calling before you even pick up the phone. It's good for screening telemarketers—another major downside to progress.

When I reached the phone company, I got a recorded message telling me to press "1" for English and "2" for Spanish. After pressing "1" I was given several options. I picked one. I was told to enter my *ten-digit* telephone number, area code first. I did that. Then came another series of choices. I punched one. I got another series of choices.

By that point, I'm screaming into the phone, "I WANT TO SPEAK TO A LIVE HUMAN BEING!," followed by a few phrases not appropriate to be repeated here. Finally, I hung up and didn't subscribe to the service I was prepared to pay extra for.

Telephone answering systems are good for off-hours to let you know when you can talk to someone about your problem. But they should be unplugged during regular office hours and replaced with warm-bodied, helpful operators who can put you in touch with the right person to answer your question or deal with your situation.

Of course, operators cost more and aren't as "efficient," if all you're looking at is the financial bottom line, as so many of today's managers do. But when it comes to customer service and satisfaction, the bottom line is that WE WANT TO SPEAK TO A LIVE HUMAN BEING!

Companies that use automatic answering services ought to be required to list as one of the options, "If you would like the company president's private line, punch 9." No doubt, you would get another answering machine, but at least you could leave a message he or she would be sure to remember.

Smoke 'Em
if You've Got 'Em

When I was growing up, we didn't hear much about how bad smoking was for our health. The surgeon general hadn't yet issued his famous warning. Most men smoked. Many women did, though not as openly.

Smoking was a nasty habit even then, but society did little to discourage it. Quite the opposite. Cigarette companies would hand out free samples on downtown streets at lunchtime. Soldiers were encouraged to "smoke 'em if you've got 'em." Cigarette ads were on TV and radio, and it was more common to see actors smoking on screen.

The phrase "second-hand smoke" was unheard of. Smokers smoked wherever they wanted to, and non-smokers pretty much had to hold their nose and live with it. At least until they became the clear majority. Back then it seemed rude for someone to ban smoking even in her own home. We have seen a major change in attitudes about smoking in my lifetime.

My dad smoked, but my mother didn't. She tolerated it, but I could tell she didn't approve. Daddy smoked a pipe, and he said he only smoked it once a day. "I light it in the morning, and I put it out before I go to bed." I have a photograph of my dad and me when I was a toddler; we both had pipes in our mouths. When I was a teen-ager, he would sneak me a couple of cigars for my buddy Jerry and me to smoke while we were out on the town.

I started smoking cigarettes when I was seventeen, right after high school graduation. The senior class in our little town went on a trip together, and the wildest thing I did was smoke cigarettes.

By college I was a regular pack-a-day smoker, and I remained at that level the first four or five years out of school. As a newspaper reporter, I came to believe that I couldn't write if I didn't have a cigarette going. Back then, of course, there was no such thing as smoke-free workplaces. Especially newsrooms.

A fellow journalist caused me to give up cigarettes. As part of a national awareness effort, he agreed to write a series

'Smoking' a corncob pipe with my dad.

of articles about not smoking for a week. I didn't intend to quit smoking, but I didn't want to add to his temptation, either. So I said I wouldn't smoke at work that week.

As it turned out, I switched to a pipe and never went back to cigarettes. He quit for the week, but resumed smoking afterwards. I didn't have a cigarette for more than twenty-five years. Then one night at a social hour, during a time of great personal stress, I smoked two cigarettes. I didn't go back to cigarettes after that, but I was hooked again. I started inhaling my pipe and my occasional cigars. At fifty-one, I had drastically, foolishly increased my chances of dying from cancer.

Several times I tried to just quit inhaling. According to the literature I've seen, pipe smoking isn't nearly as bad for you as cigarette smoking—*as long as you don't inhale.* Of course, cigarette smoking wouldn't be all that bad, I suppose, if you didn't inhale. But telling a smoker to puff but not inhale would be like telling a compulsive eater to chew but not swallow.

At any rate, I couldn't muster the discipline to stop inhaling. I had moved to a new level of smoking from which there didn't seem to be any way back. Except one.

One morning, I took a garbage sack into my smoking room and tossed in my three pipes, a pouch of tobacco, three disposable lighters, even the ashtray. I took the sack to the curb and left it for the garbage crew, then drove off to run some errands. By the time the garbage truck came, I was already having serious second thoughts.

The fact is that I didn't want to quit smoking. I enjoyed it more than ever. But every time I would light up, I would think about how bad it was for me. I would be puffing away, worrying all the while about dying of cancer. It finally came down to whether I wanted to enjoy smoking or enjoy living.

I developed strategies for trying to kick the habit. I would go for several walks a day. I started drinking more water. I reminded myself sometimes when the craving was strongest to just hang in there for five minutes. I read more. I watched more movies and ate more popcorn.

But the most successful strategy, for me, was keeping a journal. Every day or so I would write something in my journal on the computer about the experience of trying to quit or about the role of tobacco in my life. The journal helped keep me focused on the task at hand. I didn't want to admit one day in my journal that I had failed myself. The journal also gave me something to look forward to.

Sometimes I would write about how I felt about trying to quit, about how much I missed my pipe, about how relaxing it would be to sit and smoke and let my cares waft away with the smoke, but how I refused to give in to the temptation.

Sometimes I would find interesting or helpful material on the Internet or in books and include it in my journal. For example, one of the earliest warnings about the unhealthy effects of smoking came a full 360 years before the Surgeon General's Report of 1964. King James I of England in 1604 published "A Counterblaste to Tobacco" in which he wrote: "Smoking is a custom loathsome to the eye, hateful to the nose, harmful to the brain, dangerous to the lungs." In Virginia in 1619, the going rate for a wife shipped in from overseas was 120 pounds of tobacco; two years later the rate had soared to 150 pounds.

Sometimes I would write jokes or poems about smoking. (How many smokers does it take to change a light bulb? Three. One to change the light bulb while the other two take a smoke break.) *Cancer is the smoker's curse/If I might be so crude and terse./They ought to think about it first:/Their family riding behind the hearse.*

Sometimes I expressed opinions about smoking issues, such as how smoking in public places like restaurants and bars ought to be more restrictive than it is. Or how inconsistent our government policy toward tobacco has been—promoting it for years through subsidies to farmers and free samples and discounts to military personnel, and now trying to collect billions of dollars in damages from the tobacco companies.

Gradually, the journal entries became less frequent as tobacco became less a dominant force in my life. After 200 days and more than 125 pages, I declared victory and closed the book on smoking.

Now, six years later, it seems absurd to me that I ever smoked in the first place. I find it repulsive and foolish. It is absolutely the worst health habit one could choose, and yet millions continue to smoke and hundreds take up the habit every day.

I am not one to advise anyone else about how to quit smoking. After all, it took me thirty-five years to do it. But the journal worked for me, and I would recommend the approach to others who are trying to quit.

Eventually, I think tobacco use will be banned, but that will be a long time coming, probably not in my lifetime, although who could have envisioned how attitudes would change so radically about smoking in the past forty years?

Elvis and Chubby

Music changed drastically, and forever, during the '50s. Two of the principal movers and shakers of the new rock-'n'roll era became so famous that everyone knew them by their first names—Elvis and Chubby. Elvis Presley and Chubby Checker.

ELVIS

I never met Elvis, before or after his death. Elvis certainly never came to our little town, at least not in person. But in spirit he did.

We had our own Elvis impersonators. My friend, Jimmy Bass, was one. My dad, the Baptist preacher, was another.

For a youth banquet at the church, he—Daddy, not Jimmy—penciled in long sideburns, greased and tousled his hair, wore his pants down around his hips and his shirttail

My dad signing an autograph for Linda Sue Adams after his Elvis show.

out, and lip-synched the words to "Love Me Tender" and "Hound Dog."

The newspaper correspondent from our town sent a photo to the nearby city newspaper, and they printed it. Soon my dad was being castigated by the righteous, or at least the self-righteous, throughout the area. How could a preacher, a man of the cloth, condone the sinful music and even sinfuller antics of Elvis the Pelvis?

Of course, the youth in the church loved it. They thought Daddy was "cool," or whatever the term for it was then.

Later, when Elvis appeared on Ed Sullivan, somehow we managed to get to watch it, even though it was on a Sunday night.

I never was all that much of an Elvis fan, though I did first become interested in girls after watching the Elvis movie, "G.I. Blues." And I would share a special fondness with a girlfriend for one of his songs, "I Can't Help Falling in Love with You."

But my favorite Elvis wasn't Elvis at all. He was an almost forty-year-old preacher grinding his hips and giving the young people of our town an evening of entertainment, a moment to remember, and a message that life doesn't have to be taken so seriously. It's not what we imitate about life that matters. It's what we do with it.

THE TWIST

The Twist, made popular by Chubby Checker, was more than just a new dance. It was a new way of dancing.

Before The Twist, with a few exceptions, couples danced together as partners, whether the dance numbers were slow or fast, whether they danced cheek to cheek or waltzed around the room or jitterbugged. Dancing was a couple thing. You actually touched your partner.

With The Twist, however, you didn't really have to have a partner to dance. Oh, most people did dance with a partner, but it wasn't absolutely mandatory. And even if you did dance with your partner, your dance movements could be independent from each other.

That changed the way the next two generations would dance, paving the way for the disco dancing of the '70s and line and group dancing of the '90s.

I remember how self-conscious I was the first time I tried to do The Twist. I didn't know how. I didn't know the steps. But pretty soon I figured out there wasn't any right way or wrong way, and there weren't any steps. You just had to get out on the floor and go with the flow and everything would take care of itself.

Dancing was a new enough experience for me anyway, having grown up in a parsonage where dancing, while not exactly forbidden, was certainly not encouraged. I don't recall ever seeing my parents dance. Well, not together.

I do remember my mother demonstrating The Charleston one time, which was something of a forerunner of The Twist. Partners didn't have to touch to do The Charleston either, which may be why it was all right for her to show us the steps right there in the preacher's home.

Most young Baptists I knew danced, but dancing would not be sanctioned at Baptist colleges in the South for many years—and still isn't at some schools.

The Baptist attitude about dancing gave birth to a joke: Do you know why Baptists don't make love standing up? Because people might think they are dancing.

Well, The Twist changed dancing from "making love standing up" to "creative movement."

Staying Cool

We didn't have much air-conditioning when I was growing up.

Only the wealthiest few had air-conditioned homes. Our cars weren't air-conditioned. Most stores weren't even air-conditioned. Churches weren't air-conditioned.

I remember what a treat it was to step inside the bank or drug store and feel the cool blast of air-conditioning on a hot summer day. We found all kind of reasons to stop by the drug store. It was a little more difficult, especially for young boys, to come up with excuses to go to the bank, although I did go by there once when I was eight or nine to confer with the Mayor about whether I needed a permit to set up a Kool-Aid stand. He asked me where I wanted to put the stand and I said right in front of the drug store, which had a soda fountain. He laughed and said he thought that would be a fine place for my Kool-Aid stand.

The temperatures in our area typically simmered between ninety and a hundred on summer afternoons, with humidity readings to match. Looking back, I don't see how we could stand it. But, of course, at the time we didn't know how bad we had it, so we just lived with it.

Fans played a big part in our lives back then. I was particularly fond of oscillating fans—and remain so today—as much for the soothing, whirring rhythm as the cooler air. Some people had attic fans, and I can remember having to sleep under the covers—in summer even—at a friend's house because the attic fan sucked in and cooled off so much air through the open windows. Churches had cardboard fans, advertising the services of nearby funeral homes, that we could use to fan ourselves if the service got too warm.

As boys, we spent a lot of time on our bicycles, not so much because we had anywhere we needed to go (other than the drug store) but just to feel the wind in our faces. We cooled off in the town's swimming pool or in the Blue Hole swimming pond. We took advantage of shady yards and water hoses. We drank a lot of Kool-Aid and lemonade and RC Colas (because they were the biggest soft drinks). We savored Popsicles and Dreamsicles and listened for the sweet music signaling that the ice cream man's truck was in the neighborhood.

When I was sixteen, we moved into a new parsonage, and it was air-conditioned. We basked in luxury. And then we got our first electric bill! We had a family meeting and agreed that anyone leaving a room without turning off the lights would have to pay a five-cent fine. The money would be placed in a jar to help offset the cost of air-conditioning. That didn't last long and didn't make much of a dent in the utility bill anyway, but it did make the point that we needed to conserve energy, not waste it. We had to retrain ourselves to close the door behind us when we went outside.

Air-conditioning changed the way people lived in our part of the world. We spent more time indoors watching TV and less time outside playing or swimming or sitting under a shade tree or on a shady front porch sipping a cool drink and exchanging pleasantries with the neighbors. With our windows tightly sealed, we insulated ourselves to a large extent from the outside world. People could go inside their air-conditioned houses, pull the shades and live in isolated comfort if they chose.

Today we take air-conditioning pretty much for granted, as we do so many of our modern conveniences. But, unlike microwave ovens or automatic dishwashers, air-conditioning was more than just another convenience. Air-conditioning literally made life bearable in the South and Southwest, and that played a vital role in the economic and social development of those regions, aptly labeled the Sun Belt.

Downtown Revisited

In the '50s, even small towns had thriving downtowns. I look at all the empty buildings in downtowns I pass through, and I think back to the drawings they used to have in our town.

All week long when we made purchases at the local stores—Red & White Grocery, Sour Lake Drug, Brannon's Drug, Allen's Department Store, Hubbard's Department Store, Ewing Grocery, Rex Supply, the White Owl Café, White & Luce Hardware, and others—we would be given tickets for the Saturday drawings.

On Saturday downtown would be packed as everyone came to town to see if they had won the you-have-to-be-present-to-win cash drawing. Additionally, each store posted a winning number for a smaller prize. One Saturday I had the winning ticket for five dollars' worth of groceries at Red &

White and a vase at Hubbard's. You'd have thought I'd won the lottery.

Downtown back then was truly the center of town. Today it rarely is. Many small towns—the one where I grew up among them—have little commercial activity at all. And what they have may well be out on the loop that goes around town.

People think nothing of driving twenty, thirty, fifty miles to the nearest mall or Super Whatevermart, where they can get more choices at better prices. You can't blame them, and you can't blame the merchants for letting them get away. It's just a change in the way we shop.

My folks were big supporters of our community and did much of their shopping at home. But when the nearby city supermarkets started advertising huge discounts on groceries, they began making regular weekly trips to the city so they could stretch their meager dollars to better feed the family.

Some small, local businesses managed to survive by providing exceptional service, but not many. Not surprisingly, price and choice won out over service and personal relationships.

Even weekly drawings won't keep them from going to the mall these days.

What has saved—or revived—the downtowns in some communities has not been weekly drawings but a drawing of another type—drawing on the town's history or culture or charm. Every town has a story to tell, every place has some unique characteristics, but some places are better at telling it than others are.

Albany, Texas, for example, celebrates its history as a frontier outpost with an outdoor musical called "Fandangle," which involves hundreds of residents and transforms the small West Texas town into a tourist destination in June. The visitors are so charmed by the courthouse, the art center and the specialty shops that they keep coming back throughout the year.

In my hometown, a modest downtown revival has taken place in recent years as the community has embraced its colorful past. Sour Lake dates back to 1835. It was a health spa in the middle and late 1800s. Sam Houston, in his last days, went to Sour Lake for treatment in the mineral baths, only to return home and die. Sour Lake's biggest claim to fame is that it was one of the early oil boom towns. Texaco got its start in Sour Lake in 1903.

For years the history was virtually ignored. My dad would give tours of the old spa site, the Texaco monument, and the geological phenomenon known as the Sink Hole, but little was done to capitalize on the town's rich heritage. But the opening of a historical museum, the construction of a new fire station, and the restoration of a bank building as a gift shop and bed and breakfast have breathed new hope into the community.

It's a matter of pride—and money. I've seen it happen in other towns, large and small. A few people with vision and financial resources get an idea and find the support and persistence to make it happen, and that leads to another development, and pretty soon it mushrooms into a full-scale revitalization project.

Abilene's downtown renewal began with saving a historic theater and restoring an old hotel into a museum. Fort Worth's stockyards area was converted from abandoned cattle pens into a tourist center by focusing on the city's Cowtown heritage. The little town of Baird filled its empty downtown buildings with antiques and lured visitors off the interstate. Fredericksburg's old world charm brought big-city shoppers to town, which led to more shops and more visitors. Canton energized its economy by growing a flea market into a booming enterprise. Menard has taken advantage of a historic irrigation ditch and an old Spanish fort. Santa

Anna got an economic resurgence when one enterprising businessman from out of town saw a spark of potential and decided to relocate his store there.

The point is that it takes a little creativity, money and—that word again—pride. Pride in the town's heritage and character. Pride in the town's appearance. Pride in the town's potential. Some towns are blessed with it, others find ways to cultivate it, and the rest will continue to wither away.

The First
VW in Town

My dad owned the first Volkswagen in our small town. The VW Beetle, as it became known, was still very much a novelty in 1960, the era of large, high-powered cars and, not incidentally, thirty-cent gasoline. Foreign cars of any make were scarce. We still drove Fords and Chevys, even Studebakers and, briefly, Edsels.

We were driving a '57 Ford back then, one of the best cars ever, in my opinion, right up there with the '57 Chevy. But we were a one-car family, and with me now driving we were a three-driver household.

Dad was attracted to the VW for one reason: he was tight. He had to be, on a small town preacher's salary. Even at thirty cents a gallon, with all the miles he traveled going to meetings and visiting people in the hospitals, he needed to cut expenses.

The VW seemed the logical choice. It was inexpensive to buy and ridiculously cheap to operate. And since he did most of his driving by himself, he didn't need a big car.

The VW dealership, if you would call it that, consisted of a few cars on display outside a service station in Beaumont. As I remember it, you had your choice of colors as long as it was gray. We took home a gray one.

I was sixteen and had already been driving a year. But dad wasn't buying the car for me. No, this would be his work car. I would drive the '57 Ford (at least until I tore up the transmission a couple of times—but that's another story that let's not go into just now).

Daddy was proud of his Volkswagen. Everybody in town wanted to see it, and he took delight in showing it off, like the first kid on the block to have the newest toy. The engine was in the back instead of in the front like real cars.

He kept a mileage log in the glove compartment and dutifully figured the miles-per-gallon every time he filled up. It only cost three bucks to fill it, and you could drive three hundred miles or more on a tank. It didn't have a gas gauge, but if it ran out of gas, you just flipped on the reserve tank and that extra gallon would surely get you to the next service station. (We actually had *service* stations, too, where they checked the oil and the tires and swept out the floorboard when you bought gas.)

The VW became our family car. Daddy, Mother, little brother Charlie and I would cram into the car for the 600-mile round trips to San Antonio twice a year to visit grandparents. Our luggage somehow fit into the small trunk in the front, or the storage compartment in the back. It was, shall we say, cozy. But cheap. Above all, cheap.

The VW was also my choice of cars for dates or for riding around with the guys. After the newness wore off, Daddy would let me take it out. The girls thought it was cute, and the guys liked the fact that we could drive around all night for a dollar and return it with more gas than it had when we started. We could stuff eight or nine kids in there if they sat in each other's laps.

You could always find my dad because he had the only VW, maybe even the only foreign car, in town. If the VW was outside the post office, Daddy would be visiting with Plummer Barfield, the postmaster. If the VW was at the doctor's office, he would either be having his teeth worked on by Dr. Jack Ryan or taking an indigent person to Dr. Bobby Ryan for medical care. If the VW was at Merle Copeland's service station, my dad was probably telling Merle about his latest mileage figures.

One day the whole town gasped to see a gray VW in front of—well, in front of Happy Jack's beer joint. Now, my father was everybody's friend and ministered to everybody in town, and he and Happy Jack got along just fine. However, a Baptist preacher just didn't drop in for happy hour at Happy Jack's. But there was the VW, right there outside Happy Jack's at five o'clock.

That was the day Daddy learned that his pride and joy was no longer the only Volkswagen in town.

Our Love Affair
with Cars

First cars, like first loves, hold special places in our hearts.

My first car was a '57 Ford. Well, it wasn't *my* first car. It was the family car, but I was allowed to drive it when I turned fourteen and got my driver's license. On reflection, fourteen was much too young to be driving a car—especially for *me* to be driving a car—but we would never have admitted it back then.

Our '57 Ford was a column stick shift, which caused me no small measure of grief when I started driving. The driver's ed car was an automatic, and I've always preferred automatics ever since.

My father would take me out on country roads so I could get in some practice driving a stick shift since that was what

I would be driving after driver's ed ended and I was turned loose on the streets of Sour Lake. On one of our first excursions I was concentrating on the shifting so much that I had my eyes on the stick shift instead of the road, and the car drifted over onto the left side of the road. Just in time, Daddy grabbed the wheel and swerved us out of the way of an oncoming truck.

The '57 Ford wasn't air-conditioned, of course, not back then. But it had a good AM radio and it was a pretty cool car, and I drove it all the way through high school.

My own first car—the first car I actually bought with my own money—was a Corvair, later labeled by Ralph Nader as the most dangerous car on the road. Probably because I was driving.

Actually, I did total that car—but it wasn't my fault. A drunk ran a red light in Houston and that was that. I walked away with a cracked nose but nothing worse.

It wasn't my first accident, nor would it be my last. It was one of the few, however, that wasn't my fault. My brother says Dromgoole is French for "bad driver." Several generations of us stand as proof.

By the time I graduated from high school I had wrecked my dad's VW twice and the Ford once.

One of the VW wrecks could have been fatal. I went to sleep after taking a friend home out in the country one night after a track meet. I drifted off the left side of the highway and struck a wooden highway sign, which came right through the middle of the windshield and ended up in the back seat of the VW. The only way I could see that it didn't take off the right side of my head is that when I went to sleep I must have dropped my head to the left.

The next day, a Sunday, I went down to the front of the church during the invitation and tearfully "rededicated my life" to the Lord.

Cars were such an important part of our lives in the '50s, and they have been ever since. Before the '50s, few young people drove cars, much less owned their own. Post-war prosperity made us the first generation to have driver's ed and take to the streets in our cars.

Cars have been more than a means of transportation. They are image. They are impressions, attitudes, points of view. We are what we drive.

I'm not talking just about making a social statement, although cars certainly do that as well. To many people, cars are outward status symbols. More than outward appearance, however, cars affect our own feelings, how we feel inside about ourselves. I feel different about myself, for example, driving a big, red convertible with the top down than I do driving an old pickup or an economy car. I feel different in a luxury sedan than in a minivan.

In a convertible with the top down on a warm, sunny day, it's easy to be transported back quite a few years ago to when the driver and his passengers were twenty instead of, well, a bit more than twenty.

In a brand new sedan with all the extras—a car that sells for twice what he paid for his first *house*—the driver feels wealthier, more important, more conservative than he is or ought to be.

In an old VW, much like the one he grew up with, the driver finds himself feeling like a struggling artist or poet or the leader of a populist political movement.

In an old pickup with quite a few miles on it, some dents in the fender and a little mud on the flaps, the driver is convinced that even though he has never punched a dogie or a drunk, he could if he had to.

Our cars have brought much pain as well as pleasure, of course. We spend more than we should on them. They're always hungry and have to be fed. They break down when we can least afford it. They are the source of much tragedy and heartbreak.

But our generation can no more envision life without cars than the under-forty generation can envision life without TV or computers.

The Magical Windshield Wiper

In high school I helped coach a Little League team—the Yankees—for several summers. It was, I suppose, my first venture into the area of community service. Until then, I had been on the receiving end. It was time now to give back, though I'm fairly sure I didn't think of it that way at the moment.

This particular summer we had an especially enthusiastic group of eleven- and twelve-year-old boys on the team. Some groups—some teams—you just enjoy more than others. This was one of those special teams.

As a high school senior with almost constant access to the family car, it fell my duty to be the chauffeur. We put a lot of miles on the '57 Ford that summer shuttling between our little town and the ball park seven miles away.

The windshield washer on our '57 Ford was controlled by a small pedal on the floorboard. When the pedal was depressed, the washer would squirt water on the windshield, and the wipers would wipe one time, then cut off.

However, on one of our trips from the ball park, I depressed the pedal to squirt water to clean off the windshield and discovered the washer was empty. But the windshield wipers still wiped once, then turned off.

"You boys want to see my voice-activated windshield wiper?" I asked. "Look, I can just say *windshield wiper* and the windshield wiper will come on."

They were skeptical.

"Windshield wiper," I commanded. The windshield wiper wiped once, then stopped.

"How did you do that?" asked Roy, whom we had nicknamed Duck.

"I guess it's magic," I said. "It just responds to voice commands." I did it again. "Windshield wiper." It wiped once, then stopped.

Ricky thought he had it figured out. "He's pushing a button on the steering wheel." I took both hands off the steering wheel. "Windshield wiper." Wipe. Stop.

"Let me try it," Duck said. "Windshield wiper." Nothing.

"Windshield wiper," Ricky said. Wipe. Stop.

"I guess it doesn't recognize your voice, Duck," I said. "It worked for Ricky."

Sometimes it's not very hard to entertain eleven- and twelve-year-old boys. This was one of those times. I milked the windshield wiper trick the rest of the Little League season before one of the boys finally figured it out.

It's a story that comes to mind from time to time on a hot, lazy summer day, when a grown man passes by a Little League park and is reminded that, when it comes to service, those who give are the ones who truly receive.

Vote Dry!

The "wets" and the "drys" have fought in Texas for decades. Texas allows local counties, and even precincts within counties, to determine for themselves whether to allow the sale of beer, wine and liquor. There are still some counties and a good many precincts that are "dry."

The town where I grew up was "wet" as long as I can remember. But there was one election in the mid-'50s when it looked like it might go dry.

All it took to call a wet-dry election was a certain number of signatures, and that wasn't hard to come up with on such a divisive issue. The churches usually could be counted on to gather the requisite number of names on a given Sunday morning.

Of course, just because you signed the petition didn't necessarily mean that you were against booze. Signing a petition was a public declaration, and it was prudent for most small town folks to be publicly aligned against demon rum. Voting—like drinking—was, however, a private not a public matter.

On this particular campaign, the ministers in town were properly and indignantly aligned against the "wets." More than likely they were quietly encouraged by a would-be bootlegger or two who knew that they could make more money in a dry town than in a wet one.

As the Baptist preacher, Daddy was one of the leaders of the dry forces. Perhaps at that stage of his life he was privately dry as well as publicly, though that would change in time. After I reached adulthood, we would enjoy a little nightcap together, usually accompanied by a pipe or cigar.

But back then, I was ten or eleven and my dad hadn't yet come out of the closet, or the wine cellar. He helped organize a temperance parade through town to urge voters to "Vote Dry!"

It wasn't all that much of a parade, if memory serves, just a few cars and pickups with signs and streamers. Dad was driving a pickup and had several boys my age riding in the back for emotional support.

Suddenly, without consulting Daddy, one of the boys started a chant: "Vote Dry! Liquor will gitcha in TROUUUU-ble. Vote

Dry! Liquor will gitcha in TROUUUU-ble." We picked up the chant. All through town we rode, singing at the top of our voices, "Vote Dry! Liquor will gitcha in TROUUUU-ble."

Our town voted wet. Overwhelmingly wet. I don't think the drys ever tried again. I know my dad didn't.

Middle Names

Maybe this can't be proven scientifically, but I suspect that more people in small towns than in large ones, and especially in the South, were called by their first *and* middle names back in the '50s.

Among the girls in our town were Mary Ann, Mary Sue, Mary Jane, Mary Frances, Mary Lou and Mary Alice. Linda Sue, Donna Sue, Bonnie Sue, Carol Sue, Sammie Sue, Billie Sue. Linda Kay, Winnie Kay, Linda Rae, Johnnie Rae.

I knew a Bobby Wayne, Bobby Joe, Joe Bob, Joe Don, Billy Joe, Billy Bob, Billy Glenn, Billy John. James Lee, Ray Lee, Roy Lynn, Roy Lee, and Lee Roy. Joe Neal, Jo Ann, Jo Carrol, Sara Jo. Nita Lou, Linda Lou, Betty Lou. Lou Ann, Betty Ann, Beth Ann, Barbara Ann, Cheryl Ann, Carol Ann. Carol Jean, Barbara Jean, Carol May, Annie Mae, Lettie Mae.

There was Jack Wayne, Carl Wayne, Donald Ray, John Ray, John Henry. And the Earls—John Earl, Dallas Earl, Robert Earl, Henry Earl, Joe Earl. The Belles and Nells—Lula Belle, Annie Belle, Bertha Belle, Olga Nell, Adria Nell, Birdie Nell. And Frank Stanley, Minnie Lee, Martha Faye, Thelma Lois, and even a Dinkie Ruth.

Maybe I'm just more sensitive to being called by a first and middle name because growing up I was Glenn Allen. My father was Glenn, and after I left home I dropped the Allen and just became Glenn. Which made for some confusion when my dad would come to visit. He became known to my friends as The Real Glenn Dromgoole. Which made me what?

Of course, nearly all of us have middle names. But most don't have to go by them. About the only time most people get called by their first and middle names is when their mother is mad at them: "John Bradenfield Smith, you get in this house right this minute!"

Presidents are sometimes called by their first and middle names, especially when their initials are recognizable: FDR, Franklin Delano Roosevelt; JFK, John Fitzgerald Kennedy; LBJ, Lyndon Baines Johnson. Democrats stretched out Richard Milhous Nixon as a way of scolding him, I suppose, as Republicans would do with William Jefferson Clinton. The elder George Bush had two middle names—George Herbert Walker Bush.

Some people learn to part their names in the middle. It seems to be particularly prevalent among college presidents who become, say, Dr. E. Sturdivant Williams, instead of Eddie. You can be fairly certain that these people didn't grow up being called Sturdivant or Lancaster or whatever.

I worked with a man named Z. Joe, whose minister father named him for the Protestant reformer Zwingli. He answered to Joe but kept the Z. When Z. Joe's son was born, he named him Zwingli Bartholomew, or Z. Bart.

I worked with another person who went by his middle name, Rick, except he spelled it Ric. I don't know what his first name was, but it started with A. One day he had a fancy nameplate made up as A. Ric Whatever. Before long, home-made signs were springing up all over the office: A Water Fountain, A Coat Rack, A Wooden Desk, etc.

In my hometown and to my family, I am still Glenn Allen even though I've been Glenn everywhere else for nearly forty years. And so, I'm sure, are Bobby Joe, Linda Sue, Carl Wayne and Mary Alice. Dinkie Ruth, however, long ago dropped the Dinkie.

Humpy-Jack

What was your favorite toy growing up? Is there one that stands out above all the rest?

Mine was a tricycle. Not just any tricycle. The seat moved up and down as the tricycle went forward. I called it an "up-and-down tricycle." Other kids had more creative names for it, like the "Humpy-Jack."

I've never seen another one before or since. It was, I'm certain, the only up-and-down tricycle in our town. I don't know the name of the company that manufactured it, or what the tricycle officially was called. But I do have a photograph of it.

I've searched for another one at antique shops, junk stores, flea markets and old bicycle shops—to no avail. Surely more than one of the vehicles was produced.

It was bigger than most tricycles, but the feature that distinguished it was the moving seat. Riding the Humpy-Jack was sort of like riding a horse on a merry-go-round.

My up-and-down tricycle, also known fondly as the Humpy Jack.

All the kids loved to ride it. The faster you pumped, the faster it went up and down as well as forward. It was the most popular trike in the neighborhood.

I have no idea whatever happened to it. I outgrew it eventually, graduating to a bicycle, although my graduation was delayed somewhat beyond that of most boys because I had a better tricycle than they did.

My brother took it over and rode it for several more years, but neither of us can recall where it ended up after we were through with it. Our folks probably gave it to some other kid.

I've never understood why some tricycle manufacturer hasn't brought out a new version of the Humpy-Jack. Maybe today it would violate some federal safety standard.

But back then I don't remember anyone ever falling off the up-and-down tricycle, and it seemed to have universal popularity with children—at least in the limited universe I was acquainted with.

Today, of course, toys tend to be high-tech and expensive and often violent. Our kids are given too much too fast and rarely stop to appreciate what they have.

But, in all honesty, so did we. We grew up with more advantages than any generation before us, and I'm afraid that we were as selfish and as ungrateful as today's young people.

Many years later, however, I did remember to thank my parents for the up-and-down tricycle, the Humpy Jack, the best toy I ever had.

The Mud Bowl

The man across the street from where I grew up had a front yard that, to a small boy, looked as big as a football field. It didn't have any trees either, at least not in the field of play. There was the Bush That Ate Baseballs, but it was at one end and wasn't a factor in football. When I drive by that yard today, I am amazed at how *little* it seems. Maybe it has shrunk over the years.

On Sunday afternoons we would gather at my house to watch the pro football game of the week on TV—television still being something of a novelty in the mid '50s, and pro football as well. We would usually make it to the half, then we would take to the field ourselves in Mr. Hankamer's yard.

The Chisum brothers, Tolbert and Eugene, were nearly always there, as well as Jerry and Sonny and Mickey and Paul and whoever else showed up. Usually we would have three or four players to a team. We played Two-Below, which amounted to full-contact touch football. A runner or receiver wasn't down until a defender touched him with both hands below the belt.

And the game wasn't official until the Chisum brothers, who always played on opposite teams because they were the oldest and biggest and fastest and one year apart in age, took after each other with their fists. That usually happened in the first fifteen minutes. Then the game got serious—each brother playing for pride, with the teammates appropriately motivated to do so as well.

One Sunday we watched the Bears and the Giants, or maybe the Lions and Eagles, slug it out in the mud for a half, then we headed over to Hankamer Field for our own Mud Bowl. We played all afternoon in a downpour, diving for passes on the slippery turf, making sharp cuts on end sweeps only to end up face down in the mud.

History didn't record who won that game—or the outcome of the Chisum brothers' fight either—but I do remember who lost. When we trudged off the field at the end of the day, we were covered in mud from head to toe. I hosed off outside, then stripped and tossed my clothes in the washer. Sonny Mathis's mother took one look at his clothes and threw them away.

Mr. Hankamer's beautiful yard—maintained by a full-time yard man—was a sea of mud. The next day, at our parents' insistence, we apologized to Mr. Hankamer for destroying his yard. If he was upset, he managed to conceal it. His yard man went to work patching up the muddy spots, and if I'm not mistaken, Hankamer Field was ready for play again by the next Sunday.

Or maybe the Sunday after that.

Flies and Skinners

We spent hours, especially in the summer, playing flies and skinners.

I don't see kids playing that game these days. Maybe they do, but I haven't witnessed it, much less been invited to participate. I asked a young friend, who was a high school baseball player, if he played flies and skinners, and he had never heard of such a thing.

Flies and skinners is a baseball game played by any number of participants, but at least two. The batter pitches up the ball and hits it as far as he can. If a fielder catches the ball in the air (a fly) he gets three points. A clean fielding of a ground ball (a skinner) without bobbling it is worth one point. The first fielder to get nine points gets to go in and bat.

If only two people are playing, it's not a very competitive game. But it's good fielding practice. The batter hits until the

*My brother (with the glove) and I spent hours
playing baseball in the neighborhood.*

fielder collects the requisite three flies, nine skinners or
some combination thereof adding up to nine points. Then the
batter and fielder change places.

But when two or more fielders are competing for a fly or
a skinner, the game could get a bit physical, with players cut-

ting in front of each other to catch a fly ball or scoop up a grounder.

We rarely had enough players in our makeshift baseball fields for a regulation game of baseball—nine players on each side—so we played flies and skinners, work-up, straight base, and other modified and invented versions.

If we had ten or twelve players, we would probably play work-up. In work-up, three or four players would start out as batters with everyone else in the field. From the field, you had to work your way up to batter through all the various positions. As long as you kept getting a hit and running the bases, then you could continue to bat. But if you made an out, you had to go to right field and begin working your way back.

From right field, you would move to center field the next time a batter made an out. Then to left field, then third base, shortstop, second base, first base and pitcher. Sometimes we would have a catcher, but usually one of the batters had to catch when he wasn't batting.

I don't recall us keeping score during work-up even though the objective was to try to keep batting as long as possible.

Winning and losing weren't so important with either work-up or flies and skinners. It was enough to be out there on a hot summer day with a glove and a ball and a bat and a few friends, hitting, catching, throwing—playing because you loved baseball, because it was fun, because it didn't cost anything, or because there wasn't really a whole lot else to do.

A Lifetime Sport

Tennis is a lifetime sport, and I have been mediocre at it for a lifetime.

I was mediocre when I started playing at about twelve or thirteen on the three asphalt tennis courts in Sour Lake. Our school happened to hire a young tennis coach, James Schmidt, who had been a tennis star at Lamar University, which had a nationally recognized tennis program.

Mr. Schmidt would produce a number of outstanding tennis players during his brief tenure in Sour Lake. I was not one of them. I was one of the guys against whom the good players could build their confidence by consistently drubbing us.

But that was OK. I did learn the game, and that would later serve me well. I didn't play regularly for almost twenty years after high school. When I returned to the court, I found that I was still mediocre. I hadn't gotten much worse through my lack of playing. And I wouldn't get much better despite forking over several thousand dollars for lessons, club memberships, proper attire, tournament and league fees, and professionally-strung rackets.

But my re-acquaintance with tennis did put me on the court once with one of the greatest tennis players of all time, Andre Agassi.

I was living in Abilene by then. For several years we had an indoor professional tennis tournament every January. It was an exhibition tournament and didn't count in the pro standings, but the players did get paid and it was a good place for the young pro up-and-comers to get in some matches and pick up a few bucks.

We raised the money for the tournament by selling sponsorships to businesses and individuals for $250 and up. The top level of sponsorship was the pro-am. For $2,500 a company could buy a spot in the pro-am competition held the day before the pro tournament began. A representative from the company would be paired with a pro and would play at least three matches against other pro-am teams.

Our newspaper was a pro-am sponsor most years, and three times I was recruited by my boss to represent the paper on the court. Each time I protested that I was a mediocre tennis player, but the publisher would sweep aside my objection and encourage me, as the newspaper's top editor, to carry the company banner.

One year I was teamed with a player whose name has long been forgotten on the pro circuit. I picked him because at the pro-am party I had asked him what the pros hoped to get out of the pro-am matches. "Alive," he replied. That let me know that he wasn't too serious about winning and thus wouldn't be too disappointed when we didn't. So when my turn came to choose a partner, I picked Mike Whatever.

One by one the amateurs' names would be drawn from a bucket, and we would pick one of the remaining pros as our partner. The last amateur to have his name drawn that year was an accountant, Hobby Stevens, who was a pretty decent player. He had no choice as to whom his partner would be. There was only one pro left. It was a kid, not really old enough to be a pro, a kid with long, shaggy, blond hair down to his shoulders. No one had ever heard of him, and his name was hard to pronounce—Uh-GAHS-ee. Or was it AAH-gu-see? Andre Agassi.

My partner and I lost every match, including one to Agassi and the accountant, who almost won the pro-am. I don't remember how bad we got beat by them, but I never forgot either that one time in my mediocre tennis career I did manage to stay on the court for an hour or so with Andre Agassi.

I have tried to forget another encounter with tennis greatness. Again it was a pro-am. This time my name was drawn first, and I picked Robert Seguso to be my partner. Robert was ranked *number one* in the world in doubles. He and his partner, Ken Flach, would win a number of high-profile Davis Cup doubles matches.

The next morning I arrived for our first match. Of course, I was nervous about playing with the best doubles player in the world. I just hoped I wouldn't embarrass myself too much.

The pro running the tournament, Rick Meyers, gave me an unopened can of balls for us to use in our first match. I grabbed the metal tab to open the can—and sliced open my finger!

My first match with the number one doubles player in the world had to be delayed while I got first aid to stop the bleeding.

Fried Chicken

The best—absolutely the best—Sunday dinner when I was growing up was fried chicken. Second best was chicken and dumplings. But fried chicken was far and away the best.

My favorite time to eat fried chicken was when we had Dinner on the Grounds after church. Usually it came at the end of our annual spring revival, which featured a guest evangelist and a guest musician who would come to town to inspire the faithful and save souls.

The revival preachers usually stayed in our home, the parsonage, and I must say that my dad made some good choices in evangelists. Especially the preacher who brought his pistol with him and would take me out to the country for a little target practice. I thought he was pretty cool for an evangelist—a pistol-packin' preacher.

These revivals used to go two weeks, back before everybody started watching TV. Every day the evangelist would be invited

Dinner on the grounds at church.

to a different home for lunch—we called it "dinner," even though it was served at noon—and on Sunday our whole family would be invited to come along. Usually it was at Mrs. Barfield's. I'm not sure if she got to host the guest preacher on Sunday because she and her husband were the elder statesmen of the church or because she was the best cook.

Anyway, she usually fried up a platter of chicken, as I recall, but I had to be on my best behavior as the preacher's son and couldn't eat all I wanted.

The next Sunday, to either celebrate the end of the revival or a successful one or both, we had Dinner on the Grounds.

Everyone would bring a special dish for the buffet lunch, and a number of the older ladies always brought fried chicken. After all, good fried chicken is as good cold as hot. In fact, I've always figured that to be the true test of fried chicken. Since the dish would have to be brought to church before Sunday school, but wouldn't be eaten for more than two hours, it had to be something that could either be served cold (like chicken) or be heated up quickly (like green beans). This was, of course, before microwaves.

On one particularly memorable Dinner on the Grounds, when I was eleven or twelve, I engaged in a chicken-eating contest with a boy a year older named Tubby. Tubby, you might guess, was quite hefty. I was quite skinny. It seemed like a mismatch, but Tubby had not stopped to calculate how one's intense desire for fried chicken might compensate for one's lack of capacity.

We had not bothered to inform our mothers of the ensuing contest, and we were tied at eleven pieces each when they became aware of what was going on and put a stop to it. Otherwise, who knows, we might have ended up in Guinness.

My favorite pieces have always been the leg, the wishbone, and the liver. You hardly ever see a wishbone (or pulley-bone) anymore; they're just whacked up as part of the breast in the cut-up chickens you get at the supermarket. And most young cooks find the liver too yucky to fool with.

But I still eat both the wishbone and the liver, thanks to a mother-in-law who knows how to cut up and cook chicken. Her chicken is as good as any I've ever eaten, and it's as good cold as hot. She doesn't put so much batter on it, the way most commercial fried chicken places do.

Cooking fried chicken is becoming something of a lost art, it seems to me. So I consider it a patriotic, if not sacred, duty to pass along my mother-in-law's recipe. I'm sorry I can't explain how to cut it so that the wishbone is preserved as a separate piece.

Anyway, this is how Ellen, my mother-in-law, fixes chicken that anybody would be proud to take to Dinner on the Grounds.

To Fry Chicken

Wash and trim excess fat or skin from each piece and drain thoroughly. Salt and pepper to taste, then dredge pieces in flour, either in a paper bag or plastic bag. If you plan to fry the livers and gizzards, be sure to puncture them several times with a fork to prevent serious popping.

Place a generous amount of Crisco in a large iron skillet with several tablespoons of bacon drippings (if available).

When grease is very hot, add floured chicken but do not over-crowd. Cook on medium high to high heat, covered, until lightly brown, turn and continue frying until the other side is browned. Turn heat down and continue cooking until desired doneness is reached and chicken is golden brown. (Usually 15-20 minutes).

FOR CREAM GRAVY

Remove all chicken pieces from pan and pour off most of grease, leaving the brown, crispy dregs in the pan. Add small amount of flour and brown; add salt and pepper and then enough milk for as much gravy as needed. Cook on low heat to desired thickness and serve over rice, mashed potatoes or hot biscuits.

Pizza, for a Change

I love pizza. Sometimes I think I could eat it every day. But there was a time when I couldn't stand it.

That was a long time ago, when I was in high school and pizza was just beginning to be recognized, in our part of the country at least, as an American dish.

We didn't have any thirty-minute delivery guarantees, or even any deliveries at all. In fact, in our town you couldn't get pizza. But there was one place in the nearby big city—an Italian restaurant on the traffic circle—that served it. I remember going there with some friends, and they ordered pizza. I thought it was the worst smelling stuff in the world. How could anyone eat it?

Somewhere down the line my ideas about pizza changed to the point where not only am I not offended by the smell of it, I genuinely like the smell, as well as the taste.

The point here is not really about pizza at all, but about change. We all change our minds about things, not just inconsequential matters like the smell of pizza, but important things. Or at least we should.

We are exposed to new ideas, new places, new people, new tastes, and we change some of our earlier preconceived notions. Education and travel expose us to more of the world—different ways of living, different styles, different customs, different foods, different languages, different points of view, different outlooks on life. New experiences broaden us, whether it's climbing a mountain, or riding a subway, or visiting a nursing home, or taking in a rock or symphony concert, or going deep-sea fishing, or delivering meals to poor or elderly people.

It can be frightening, this business of change, because we are dealing with the unfamiliar, the unknown. We are comfortable with what we know and uncomfortable with what we don't know, and that can be unsettling.

And yet, in the long run, we should be more frightened by the lack of change because it means we are becoming stagnant, we are getting complacent, we aren't learning, we've stopped growing.

That's not to say that all change is good. It isn't. But it is a fact of life. Things change. We change. How we deal with change determines, to a large extent, how satisfied we will be with our lives.

Pass the pizza.

A Small Town
in Texas

I grew up in a small town. I like small towns. I thought I would always live in a small town.

I like the informality of small towns, where everyone knows everyone else, where the church and the school are the center of community life, where the whole town turns out for the football game or the school play.

Small towns are good places to grow up in. Certainly that was my experience in Sour Lake, a small town in the southeast corner of the state near Beaumont, and it remains a common theme among promoters and defenders of small town life.

So, if I like small towns so much, why have I lived in cities most of my adult life? My story may be fairly typical of others who have left these towns. I'm part of the reason for the population decline of small towns—me and the millions like me who migrated to the bigger cities in search of, well, mostly better-paying jobs.

That is what small town leaders typically say is the reason for so many younger people leaving. There just aren't enough good jobs to keep them home. But I suspect that isn't the whole problem. At least it wasn't in my case. A big part of my leaving had to do with career plans, but not all of it.

When I left Sour Lake to go away to college, I fully intended to come back. I thought I would take over the town's newspaper, help build a better community, and maybe win the Pulitzer Prize along the way.

After college I went off to the city to work for a big newspaper, thinking that I would get a couple of years' experience before settling down with my weekly. I never went back.

I learned that I rather liked the anonymity and the freedom a larger city affords. When everyone knows everyone, everyone's business becomes everyone's knowledge.

In the small town where I grew up, I felt I was always having to live up (or down) to someone else's expectations or aspirations or reputations, based not on who I was but on who my family was. In the city, whether I made it or not depended a lot more on my own endeavors, my own talents, my own initiative.

I don't mean to downplay the importance of a good upbringing, but when you grow up in a place—especially in a small town—you're always so-and-so's son or daughter. Some people find that to be stifling.

I also found that I thrived on the professional associations in the city. If I had edited my own weekly, I would have worked virtually alone, or with a very small staff. I had come to realize how important it was to me to be around talented writers and editors I could learn from and depend on.

I enjoyed the satisfaction of writing a story I knew would be read by thousands of people, instead of a few hundred. I liked the challenge of helping produce a daily paper. And while I wasn't getting rich, I was earning a lot more money that I could have expected to in a smaller town.

By the time my two years were over, I wasn't ready to leave. And while the idea of moving back to a small town still crosses my mind from time to time, it's probably just a fantasy, as it is for many who made that migration.

We're the generation who left, whether for opportunity, for freedom, or just because it was the road leading out of town. The world was changing out there and we wanted to see more of it and be part of it.

Maybe the next generation will be the one that stays or comes back to the smaller towns—in search of those same traditional values our generation ran away from, but with new opportunities for career development made possible by widely available and ever-changing technology.

Small town life isn't for everyone. But if young adults can find ways to earn a decent living and achieve professional and personal fulfillment, more of them might see it as a viable option for their families.

At a reunion of my high school class, we were each called on to say something. I said it was a great place and a great time in which to grow up. For me, it was. For others, I hope it will continue to be.

Where Are
You From?

It's a question we're not as apt to be able to answer anymore.

Where are you from?

I've always been able to say "I'm from Sour Lake" because I was born there, grew up there, finished high school there, continued to go back there most of my life because my parents lived there. My roots are there.

These days I'm more likely to say "I live in Abilene" because I've lived there for nearly twenty years and I have family and friends there.

But when people ask my daughters "Where are you from?" how can they answer? They were born in one city, finished high school in another town where neither of their parents live anymore, and they live in points distant. Best they can do, I suppose, is say "I'm from Texas" even though they no longer reside there either.

The "where are you from" question goes to more than just geography. Where are you from politically? Where are you from professionally? Where are you from theologically? Where are you from genealogically? Where are you from academically? Where are you from athletically? Where are you from musically?

It's not so simple anymore. We used to be from the country, or from a town, or from the city. We grew up, and stayed with, our parents' politics and theology. We knew our family tree, or at least most of the branches. We were Aggies or Longhorns or Sooners or Fighting Irish. We were Yankees or Dodgers or Cardinals or Cubs. We were rock'n'roll or classical or country.

These days we're mobile, fragmented, specialized, independent. We have so many choices, so many possibilities, so many channels, so many web sites. Our communities of interest, our hamlets of association, our places of the heart cross geographical, political, racial, philosophical boundaries.

It's not all bad, these choices, these opportunities, this openness, this independence. But when someone asks

"Where are you from?" what do we say?

Maybe it's a question that eventually no one even bothers to ask.